IS THE COMINTERN COMING BACK?

Essays on Party Development
98-1

A project of
The Center for Party Development

Wallace H. Spaulding

With a Foreword by
Ralph M. Goldman

University Press of America,® Inc.
Lanham • New York • Oxford

Copyright © 1998
University Press of America,® Inc.
4720 Boston Way
Lanham, Maryland 20706

12 Hid's Copse Rd.
Cummor Hill, Oxford OX2 9JJ

Library of Congress Cataloging-in-Publication Data

Spaulding, Wallace H.
Is the Comintern coming back? : essays on party development 98-1 :
a project of the Center for Party Development / Wallace H.
Spaulding.
p.   cm.
Includes bibliographical references and index.
1. Communist parties. 2. Communist strategy. 3. World politics—
1989- I. Title.
HX44.5.S7   1998   320.53'2 —DC21   98-9575 CIP

ISBN 0-7618-1062-5 (cloth: alk. ppr.)

Contents

Foreword

Ralph M. Goldman

The objective of this meticulously researched study is *not* to restart the Cold War, but rather to demonstrate that communists are still with us, and where. Wallace Spaulding authoritatively describes their organizing standards, their competing centers of factional activity, their overlapping affiliations, and their global reach. If nothing else, communists are organization people. They have been organization people for over 150 years. They will be with us for centuries to come. They are the archetypical transnational political party. And they will pursue confrontation with the democracies at the same time that they capture the symbols of their non-communist opponents—democracy, peace, people—in their titles and rhetoric. The interpretation of international behavior and the making of United States foreign policy requires that we be cognizant of the perspective of a potential competitor, particularly a revived and renewed Comintern.

By carefully tracking the intricate and often subtle connections among major and minor Marxist party organizations, by relating parties to front organizations, and by identifying the profile of contemporary factionalism within the international communist movement, Spaulding finds that one major faction relates to Kim Chong-il of North Korea, another to the French Communist Party, and a third to the middle-of-the-road publication *Links*. We learn which faction is Left, which Center, and which Right. We quickly see why Fidel Castro is hardly "isolated," as widely thought by

U.S. analysts, and will probably continue to flourish as a hero of the movement. We see unnoticed connections to Hafiz al-Assad, understand better his intransigent negotiating style, and appreciate why he is so tricky a player in the Middle East peace process. We learn that, despite their often tiny membership and bizarre names, the Communist movement's fringe groups are still international, are working hard to develop an organizational infrastructure, and are nevertheless carrying on with factions and deceptions as of old. Tactically, they are pragmatic, even willing to compete in the electoral arena as they rebuild their organizations and credibility.

The good news is that several other transnational parties have emerged over the past half century that are democratic and anti-communist competitors: the Christian Democrat International, the Socialist International, the Liberal International, the International Democrat Union or Conservative International, and lesser others. These are primarily loosely organized confederations of national parties. As supranational organizations such as the United Nations and the European Union evolve, so do the transnationals, with growing but yet unseen significance. The revival of an equivalent of the Comintern, a substantial likelihood, would undoubtedly motivate these democratic transnationals to shift into high gear.

The bad news is that the communist penchant for conspiracy, dictatorship, and violence will probably impede the world's progress toward democracy and an era of freedom and equality for all peoples. This may also distort the development of a transnational party system as the institutional alternative to warfare. The democratic transnationals will have their alertness and skills in global policy debates fully tested, which will itself be a problem of teaching old dogs new tricks.

Political parties become transnational when they develop organizations that cooperate in a variety of ways across national boundaries. Transnationals meet several of the definitional requirements of all political parties, for example, formality of organization (officers, central headquarters, publications, etc.), overtness of activities, and specificity of programs. The membership of the major transnational parties consists of national parties, national and international observer groups, and, occasionally, functional organizations (trade union, women, youth, students, etc.) and individual persons. Where international or supranational governmental agencies exist, transnational parties are likely to nominate their party leaders for official positions in these agencies, as in the case of the European Union.

Transnational parties engage in several kinds of activities typically found in pluralistic national party systems:

1. Election of party leaders to public offices.
2. Coordination of transnational party programs, as may be seen in the work of Party Groups of the European Parliament. Each major European transnational party represented in the Parliament has its own caucus-type organization, the Party Group, whose staff prepares policy studies on the issues before the Parliament.
3. Promotion of compatible national party organizations and encouragement of their affiliation to the transnational party.
4. Coordination of political operations in supranational agencies such as the European Union and its Parliament, the Organization of African Unity, the Organization of American States, and the United Nations.

Christian Democrats

Christian democracy emerged in the nineteenth century as an antagonist of liberalism which was the dominant ideology of that era. Christian Democrats also opposed the centralizing tendencies of nineteenth century nation-states. The movement was steeped in Catholic theological principles and was particularly active in local politics. In the early years of the twentieth century, as Christian Democrats gained stature and office in Europe, significant changes began to appear in their policy orientations.

After the Second World War, these parties, under the rubric of Nouvelles Equipes Internationales, set aside their Catholic emphases, were elected to national office throughout Europe, began to gain influence in Latin America, and devoted attention to transnational organization.

Although first efforts at international Christian Democratic cooperation were initiated in 1919, it was not until 1940 that an International Democratic Union was organized. It included many European governments-in-exile. In July, 1947, an international congress established the International Union of Christian Democrats. This became the Christian Democratic World Union in 1961.

Today, the Christian Democrat International (the new name adopted in 1982) has 64 member parties, 22 associated parties, and 17 observer groups. There are several affiliated organizations: Christian Democrat Feminine International; Christian Democrat Organization of America; Christian Democratic Workers International; European People's Party;

European Union of Christian Democrats; and International Union of Young Christian Democrats.

Some Christian Democratic parties are much more conservative than others, and, instead, have become associated with the conservative International Democrat Union, as indicated below.

Socialists

Although the Socialist International may be regarded as a direct descendant of earlier Marxist internationals, socialists inaugurated an entirely new organization after the Second World War. Specifically, on March 5, 1945, at the invitation of the British Labour Party, the First Conference of Social Democratic Parties, with thirteen parties represented, gathered in London for the purpose of planning the founding of a new international. By 1951, a new Socialist International came into being.

According to recent count, the Socialist International recently claimed a membership of 80 member parties (which does not include the 34 added in 1996), 31 consultative parties, 18 observer parties, and several fraternal organizations: Asia-Pacific Socialist Organization; International Falcon Movement-Socialist Educational International; International Federation of the Socialist and Democratic Press; International League of Religious Socialists: International Union of Socialist Democratic Teachers; International Union of Socialist Youth); Jewish Labor Bund; Labor Sports International; Party of European Socialists; Socialist Group of the European Parliament; Socialist International Women; Socialist Union of Central and Eastern Europe; and World Labor Zionist Movement.

In the 1950s and 1960s, a major concern of Socialist parties was containment of communism. Historically, most social democrats and laborites have advocated nonviolent change within the context of parliamentary systems and have been consistent in their opposition to totalitarian political methods. Left-wing socialists, however, have often sought "united fronts" of all fellow-Marxists as a political tactic, and may be doing so again. In 1969, under the leadership of Chancellor Willy Brandt, West German socialists adopted an *Ostpolitik* strategy of rapprochement with the Soviet Union and Eastern Europe. This carried over into Brandt's leadership of the Socialist International in the 1970s, during which there prevailed a kind of detente between Socialists and Communists.

In recent practice, the Socialist International (SI) favored firmness in dealings with European communists. Following the collapse of the Berlin

Wall in 1989, most former communist parties in Eastern Europe renamed themselves as socialist or democratic, but, by 1996, only three (in Hungary, Poland, and Slovakia) had achieved full member status in the SI (as had the formerly communist party in Italy) in Western Europe. The SI has been notably more lenient in Latin America, where three of its full members (in Chile, Nicaragua, and Paraguay) and three of its consultative ones (in Dominica, Venezuela, and St. Kitts-Nevis—the latter ruling) signed the radical 1992 Pyongyang Declaration (see Chapter 2, below), hardly a sign of democratic orientation.

Liberals

Liberals were the major ideological force in Europe during the nineteenth century, representative of commercial and industrial interests in particular. International conferences of liberals made their first appearance in 1910, but not until April, 1947, did liberals take steps toward transnational organization.

On April 14, 1947, representatives of nineteen liberal parties and groups, mainly European, signed a Liberal Manifesto in Oxford, England, which became the basic document of the World Liberal Union, or Liberal International.

The Liberal International was mainly European in its membership and policy concerns until the Canadian Liberal Party joined in the early 1970s. Thereafter, the leadership of the Liberal International began to focus on issues of a global rather than a Eurocentric perspective and also began to reach out to organized liberals on other continents. Nineteenth century ideological doctrines were either dropped or modernized by the Declaration of Oxford in 1967 and the Liberal Appeal of 1981.

Growth in the number of member parties has been impeded by the minority status of Liberal parties in many countries. There are currently approximately 40 member parties and 22 observer groups in the Liberal International. Affiliated organizations include: Committee of Liberal Exiles; Federation of Liberal and Centrist Parties of Central America and the Caribbean; Federation of Liberal, Democratic and Reform Parties of the European Community; International Federation of Liberal and Radical Youth, and the National Democratic Institute for International Affairs.

Conservatives

The most recently established transnational is the International Democrat Union, an outgrowth of the European Democrat Union (EDU). EDU was active during the first direct elections of representatives to the European Parliament in 1979. The principal European members are the British Conservative Party and the German Christian Democratic Party.

In 1983, the Reagan-Bush administration took the lead in organizing a Pacific Democrat Union. This was followed by creation of the International Democrat Union (IDU), incorporating both EDU and PDU. Subsequently, a Caribbean Democrat Union (CDU) was formed as an affiliate of IDU. Similar efforts were undertaken to create regional IDU associations in Central and South America and in the Middle East.

Fifty-seven national parties are now members of IDU. In addition to the above organizations (EDU and CDU), other affiliates include: Democratic Youth Community of Europe; European Democratic Students; European Medium and Small Business Union; European Union of Women; and International Young Democrat Union.

Communists

The oldest of the transnationals were the communist internationals that for more than a century promoted the violent overthrow of bourgeois governments. Today, the communists do not have a formal transnational organization. Instead, they continue to conduct, among other activities, international festivals and conferences, often under the auspices of the French Communist Party and the Korean Workers' Party, as Wallace Spaulding describes in this book.

The movement began as the International Working Men's Association, or First International, of 1864. In 1889, a coalition of trade unions, reformist Marxist parties, and revolutionary groups merged to become the Second, or Socialist Worker's, International. This organization reached into twenty-three countries. The Second International disbanded during World War I. The founding congress of the Third International (the Comintern) convened in Moscow in March 1919.

The Bolshevik Revolution of 1917 in Russia established the first Communist-controlled government. The Communist Party of the Soviet Union (CPSU) thereafter became the world organizing center for the new transnational party. The Bolsheviks declared themselves the vanguard of a movement that would eventually establish a communist world order. The

The Bolshevik Revolution of 1917 in Russia established the first Communist-controlled government. The Communist Party of the Soviet Union (CPSU) thereafter became the world organizing center for the new transnational party. The Bolsheviks declared themselves the vanguard of a movement that would eventually establish a communist world order. The communists have always seen theirs as a *world* party movement and precursor of a *world* political system in the Marxist-Leninist mold.

The Comintern was officially disbanded in 1943 as a gesture of friendship toward the Allies in the common fight against the Axis. In 1947, however, a Communist Information Bureau (Cominform) was established by representatives of Communist parties in nine countries of Europe.

Over the next three decades, the world Communist movement experienced fluctuating fortunes. Tito of Yugoslavia was expelled from the Cominform in 1948 for advocating "separate roads" to socialism. A decade later a breach between the Soviet and Chinese parties initiated an era of Sino-Soviet tension that only recently has begun to dissipate. In 1956, the Cominform was disbanded. In 1957, the Soviet Union made an unsuccessful attempt to reestablish the Comintern or some equivalent organization. By 1960, Maoism became a leading force in the Third World. By 1975, Eurocommunists in Italy and France were beginning to distance themselves from Moscow-centered policies and programs.

At the time of the great political upheavals in Eastern Europe and the former Soviet Union in 1989, there were well over a hundred Communist parties. Those formally recognized by the Soviet Union existed in some 95 countries. Their variety—Titoist, Maoist, Trotskyist, Eurocommunist, etc.—was testimony of the movement's factionalism.

At the present time, there is no formal communist transnational party organization, although there is little diminution in the number of national communist and related parties still extant that conduct business of one kind or another. This is what this book is about.

United States Involvement

The two major parties of the U.S. are presently also members of transnational parties. With the encouragement of then Vice President George Bush, in 1983-1984 the Republican Party helped create the International Democrat Union, that is, the Conservative International. Republicans continue to cooperate with IDU through the work of the International Republican Institute (IRI). Somewhat more cautious, the Democratic Party's National Democratic Institute for International Affairs (NDIIA) accepted membership in the Liberal International as an observer group. IRI and NDIIA are the principal agencies in the United States' democratization program; their special task is to assist in overseas development of democratic party systems.

Under the democratization program, IRI and NDIIA perform a U.S. foreign policy function by providing technical political aid to countries with emergent party systems and to those making a transition from authoritarian rule to democracy. These aid activities have produced achievements well beyond their budgetary outlays.

IRI and NDIIA are associated with their respective party national committees. Both institutes currently receive part of their funding from Congressional appropriations to the National Endowment for Democracy. Both IRI and NDIIA also raise funds through individual contributions, grants from private foundations, projects sponsored by the Agency for International Development, and special fund-raising events. Often in the past, when Congress debated the annual appropriation for the National Endowment for Democracy (NED), the debates revealed deep suspicion of NED, NDIIA, and IRI. However, with the passage of time, there has been growing understanding and enthusiasm for the work of the two institutes.

The model for a systematic approach to political aid was forged in West Germany where, soon after World War II, the Bundestag (Parliament) began to appropriate public funds in support of the domestic civic educational work of special political foundations (*Stiftungen*). After a time, the political foundations acquired a further mission, namely, to extend their democratization activities to politically compatible partners in foreign nations, particularly in the Third World. In doing so, each German party foundation worked with its natural ally among the transnational parties: Christian Democratic, Socialist, Liberal, or, more recently, Greens.

The *Stiftungen* approach was adopted by Americans looking for methods of implementing a similar kind of political aid. During the mid-1970s, George E. Agree, a Washington political consultant, conducted a project—Transnational Interactions of Political Parties—sponsored by Freedom House of New York City. This led to creation of an American version of the *Stiftungen*, namely, the American Political Foundation (APF). In 1982, the Reagan Administration gave an initial grant of $300,000 to the American Political Foundation for a six-month study to develop proposals for a democracy program.

When the study group submitted its report on April 18, 1983, it recommended not only the creation of a private, nonprofit National Endowment for Democracy, but also nongovernmental institutes to be set up by the Democratic and Republican parties, the AFL-CIO, and the U.S. Chamber of Commerce. These institutes were to receive their funds through the National Endowment for Democracy.

Thus, in this indirect fashion, U.S. parties have become involved in the civic educational functions of the major transnational parties. The transnationals themselves have grown in numbers and influence. Only the Comintern seems to be defunct. Wallace Spaulding's work tells us otherwise.

Introduction

Since 1919, the far Left—the communist parties of the world and their allies—had been coordinated and controlled to a large extent by the Communist Party of the Soviet Union (CPSU). (An early exception, relevant to this study, was the founding of the Trotskyist Fourth International in 1938.) Since the period between the 1989 destruction of the Berlin Wall and the 1991 demise of the Soviet Union, the far Left has become increasingly fragmented and polycentric. The political party and front organizational elements of the old system have more or less remained intact, although in many cases weakened.

What is new is the emergence of three international centers, each with a different ideological orientation and function. The functional differences help explain the fact that the adherents of each center often overlap with one or, more rarely, two of the others. The overlaps give the extreme Left a vague sort of unity, but one certainly not reminiscent of the pre-1991 era.

The CPSU had furnished, if not imposed, ideological leadership, which it channelled through interparty and front organization conferences and an international periodical. Today, we have the North Koreans self-consciously promulgating doctrine, the French Communist Party (PCF) as the most visible promoters of the conference system (at least at the multiparty level), and the Australian-based and Trotskyist-flavored *Links* magazine as the most strinking international publication for promoting Marxism.

These three centers, respectively, manifest relative ideological tendencies of Left, Right, and Center within the overall far Left spectrum. This is graphically illustrated in Denmark, where not one of the three signers of the radical North Korean Pyongyang Declaration (1992) was a member of the *Links*-approved, four-party Red-Green Alliance. Nor did either group include the relatively Rightist Socialist People's Party chosen by the PCF to represent the country at a select meeting of West European "progressives" held in Paris in June 1996.

In brief, the Pyongyang Declaration is a call for "all progressive political parties, organizations and peoples of the world" to strive to "defend socialism against capitalism and imperialism." "The socialist movement . . . should not abandon its revolutionary principles at any time or under any circumstances, but uplift the banner of socialism." The diatribe and rationale are familiar ones drawn directly from the communist lexicon.

Countervailing tendencies toward communist unity could be seen in the fact that representatives from all three of these Danish groupings attended the PCF's 1992 *L'Humanite* newspaper festival. This latter phenomenon made such festivals close in function to the traditional international communist front organizations. For example, representatives from all three of these Danish groups also participated in the 1986 Copenhagen "World Congress Devoted to the International Year of Peace," the last of the massive old-style conferences promoted by the communist-front World Peace Council (WPC).

Worldwide cohesiveness is provided by the overlap of the 235 signers of North Korea's Pyongyang Declaration and the some 250 participants in the major PCF-sponsored conferences during the 1990-1997 period. Only some 50 parties make up this overlap, which include the contiguous ruling parties of Angola and Namibia and the *de facto* junior governing partner of South Africa (that is, that country's Communist Party), the two large communist parties in India (one of which has ruled the populous state of West Bengal for 20 years), and the major communist party of Russia.

One is more impressed, however, by the exclusivity between Pyongyang Declaration signers and PCF-conference participants. The substantial number of parties *not* overlapping implies that there is indeed a rivalry between the two centers. Strikingly, not one of the other governing communist parties still ruling—in China, Cuba, Laos, and Vietnam— signed the Pyongyang Declaration, but each, with the exception of Laos, participated in the 10 PCF conferences tabulated in Appendix II. Laos participated six times.

Similarly, not only did the traditional Eurocommunists of Italy, Japan, Mexico, and Spain, regardless of their present organizational guise, avoid signing the Pyongyang Declaration, but this was also true of the semi-Eurocommunist PCF and Stalinist Portuguese Communist Party. Each participated in all 10 of the PCF conferences cited, with the exceptions of the [now Socialist] Italian Democratic Party of the Left (which, nevertheless, attended five) and the [communist-included] Mexican Revolutionary Democratic Party (which attended two).

The other striking pattern of factional separation is in East European countries, where a strong, reformed communist party, usually calling itself socialist, participates in the PCF system only, while a small, more radical Left wing party, retaining the communist title in its name, has signed the Pyongyang Declaration only. The exception is in Hungary, where the Declaration-signing Leftist group not only participates in the PCF system, but has done so more consistently than its larger, "socialist" counterpart.

Left unity is most apparent in Latin America. One series of communist party conferences appears to have rivalled a much more comprehensive and powerful Left series a la Eastern Europe. These two conference series would seem to fall out along North Korean versus PCF lines. However, such a strict division seems to have been mitigated to some extent by the following circumstances. Nearly half the main line, traditional communist parties of the region—and over half of those that are still "going concerns"—signed the Pyongyang Declaration *and* participated in the PCF system. The communist parties appear to be included in the more comprehensive Left meetings, where they exercise influence consistent with their usually rather limited strength at home.

Cuba is the friend of all at these conferences. Elements all along the Left spectrum appear to be enthusiastic participants in Cuban support activities. Since 1990, all this seems to have made the broad Left grouping and its almost annual meetings of the Sao Paulo Forum the world's biggest contemporary success story for Left unity. The Sao Paulo Forum now has a permanent headquarters in the city of the same name.

It is the continuing Leftist strength in various countries of Latin America as well as the parties' flexibility that makes the Forum so important. Two of its major actors—the chief opposition parties in El Salvador and Nicaragua—are Pyongyang Declaration signers that not only participate in the PCF conferences, but also serve on the *Links* magazine staff. Two others—the ruling Cuban Communist Party (possibly) and the major Leftist force in Brazil (definitely)—also have *Links* contributing editors and at the same time participate in the PCF system. The final two of these Forum "powers"—the Number 3 parties of Mexico and Uruguay—participate only in the PCF and the North Korean systems, respectively.

The importance with which the Forum is regarded worldwide is evident from the communist party observers who attend and the top billing it receives in *Links* magazine. Observers have been sent by the communists of China, France, North Korea, and India.

The Forum's ability to reach into the Left Center (?) is seen in its co-option of the ruling parties of Haiti and Panama onto its Working Group in 1993 and 1994, respectively. The most striking examples of Left-Center co-optation, however, have been in another region: South Asia. There, the until recently ruling and "moderate" party of Pakistan had, inexplicably, signed the radical Pyongyang Declaration. And, the normally ruling party of India (equally "moderate"), less surprisingly, sent its secretary general to the 1994 PCF Congress. Note that both of these parties had representatives at the previously noted 1986 Copenhagen World Congress Devoted to the International Year of Peace.

This book proposes to document the status of the world communist scene as sketched out above, identify the significant connections between its components, and speculate on the implications for transnational party development.

Chapter 1

Background: Primarily a Soviet-Dominated System (1919 to 1991)[1]

Background

The modern international communist movement was officially launched at the First Communist International (Comintern) Congress of March 1919. This meeting drew delegates from thirty countries, of which only nine had *bona fide* communist parties.[2] The Comintern organizational structure, with periodic meetings of its governing bodies (congress, executive committee, and presidium), international bureaucracy in Moscow (political secretariat, political commission, subordinate country secretariats, and related bodies), its *Communist International* newspaper, its agents and agencies abroad, and its auxiliary organizations, all served as mechanisms through which the Soviet Union controlled the international movement.

Unlike the situation later, communist parties of this initial era had no independent existence either in theory or in fact. Each was a national section of the Comintern. Also, unlike later, the Moscow control apparatus was an international one in which non-Russian party representatives occupied high positions, although later gradually excluded from any real authority.[3]

The significant early power struggles within the Comintern were basically between and among Russians, e.g., Stalin versus, first, the Trotsky-Zinoviev bloc and, then, against Comintern Secretary General Nikolai Bukharin.[4] The non-Russian struggles within the movement were sometimes real and sometimes an imagined ripple effect of something else. For example, between 1924, the time of Lenin's death, and 1930, Stalin used the Comintern apparatus to replace the allegedly Trotskyist leadership of one national communist party after another.[5]

There were also striking similarities between the Comintern era (1919-1943) and the period from the 1950s through the 1980s. The Comintern apparatus had country desks or secretariats that followed the day-to-day activities of the various foreign communist parties. The same type of structure, with some similarity in country groupings, existed in the latter period within the CPSU, by then made up entirely of Soviet personnel. This generalization applied specifically to its International Department (for non-governing communist and other parties) and its Department for Relations with the Communist Parties of Socialist Countries.[6] One author regards the CPSU Foreign Affairs Department as the common ancestor of these two bodies and as the direct successor of the Comintern. He dates its formation as 1943, the year of the Comintern's dissolution.[7]

The stationing of International Department representatives in certain Soviet embassies abroad in the post-World War II[8] era was similar to the previous Comintern system of sending direct emissaries for on-the-spot monitoring of non-Russian communist parties.[9] The Comintern's regional bureaus abroad, i.e., Western Europe, Latin America, and the Far East,[10] were (and are) paralleled by regional communist party conferences. Most strikingly, the seven Comintern congresses held between 1919 and 1935 were directly imitated by the three world communist party conferences held in 1957, 1960, and 1969 in that they were staged to demonstrate universal communist acceptance of predetermined Soviet policy lines.[11]

The Comintern's *Communist International* was a Soviet-dominated purveyor of the party line. It was followed in this function by *For a Lasting Peace, for a People's Democracy* (Cominform Journal) during 1947-56 and *Problems of Peace and Socialism* (*World Marxist Review*) during 1958-90.

The Communist Information Bureau (Cominform), besides publishing the newspaper, served as the sole visible unifying structure for a limited international communism. It existed from 1947, the year of the first of the post-World War II world communist party conferences. As such, the Cominform became symbolic of, first, the launching of Cold War postures by the Soviet side (1947) and, then, the Soviet attacks against Tito (1948). Subsequently, the Soviets' dissolution of the Cominform in 1956 was associated with an attempted rapprochement with Tito[12], just as the previous discontinuance of the Comintern in 1943 had been with an attempt to improve relations with the World War II allies.[13]

Although its newspaper covered the world, the Cominform was strictly a European organization, having its headquarters in Belgrade and, later, in Bucharest. Its membership was limited to the major European communist parties. Its energies were concentrated on limiting American influence in Western Europe, at the same time ensuring Soviet control over the eastern part of the continent. Stalin's engineering of purges of alleged Titoists in Czechoslovakia, Bulgaria, Hungary, and Poland during this period indicated that the autonomy granted national communist parties at the time of the Comintern's dissolution was not meant to be the real thing.[14]

Several of the Comintern's auxiliary organizations—the Communist Youth International, the Red International of Labor Unions, the International Peasant's Council, and the discontinued Communist Women's Organization—directly paralleled post-World War II Soviet-line international communist fronts. These were, respectively, the World Federation of Democratic Youth (WFDY), the World Federation of Trade Unions (WFTU), the Trade Union International (TUI) of Agricultural, Forestry, and Fishery Workers, and the Women's International Democratic Federation (WIDF). Whereas the older organizations were official affiliates of the Comintern,[15] the later ones were, at least until 1991, coordinated to some extent by the Soviets relatively overtly, but unofficially, through a common link with still another front, the World Peace Council (WPC). Also, there was relatively covert coordination through the CPSU International Department (see below). The common aim of both sets of organizations remained the same: to expand support for Soviet policy objectives beyond that already committed to by communist parties, making full use of the latter in this objective.[16]

In sum, there was a clear transnational organization structural outline for the world's communists. Control ran from the CPSU leadership to the system manipulated first by the Comintern and then, later, by the party foreign departments. Under the latter, the Cominform, for a time, and the WPC played important intermediary roles during the post-World War II era.

The "World Revolutionary Process" and Its Component Parts

Soviet ideologues spelled out in great detail the components of what they considered the progressive and inevitably triumphant force in world history, a force they called the "World Revolutionary Process."[17] This process was said to be carrying forward the basic transformation of our times, namely, "the transition from capitalism to socialism."[18] In opposition to this world revolutionary process was "world capitalism," especially in its most advanced "state monopolist" and "imperialist" forms.[19]

The "World Communist Movement" was the names used by Soviet writers to classify the collectivity of communist parties that *they* recognized as such.[20] These were usually limited to one per country and, for those parties formed since the Sino-Soviet split, to pro-Soviet parties. Anti-Soviet parties of various hues were also recognized in those countries where they existed before the post-World War II splits in the movement. This was done particularly for countries where no viable pro-Soviet counterpart had emerged. The world communist total of 77 million adherents claimed by Soviet writers in 1981 must have included the 39 million listed by the Chinese.[21] In 1988, the claim was 85 million, of whom 46 million were Chinese.[22] Throughout the 1981-88 period, Soviet writers declared that there were communist parties in 93 or 94 countries,[23] with an authoritative pronouncement in 1988 that gave full recognition to two parties each in India, Senegal, and Sweden.[24]

Soviet writers referred to the countries governed by communist parties as constituting the "World Socialist System."[25] A subdivision of this category—to denote those ruling parties that generally followed Russian leadership—became necessary when certain parties began to resist the traditionally subordinate role. This subdivision, called the "Socialist Commonwealth," was identified by Brezhnev in his speech to the 26th CPSU Congress (February 1981) and included the USSR, Bulgaria, Cuba, Czechoslovakia, the German Democratic Republic, Hungary, Laos, Mongolia, Poland, Romania, and Vietnam.[26]

It is assumed that Cambodia was added to the above roster at the time of the May 1981 formal reestablishment of a pro-Soviet ruling party in that country. Unlike its North Korean counterpart in Asia, Romania was apparently included because it had not withdrawn completely from such institutional arrangements as the Council for Mutual Economic Assistance (CMEA or COMECON) or the Warsaw Pact. The other ruling parties excluded from the Socialist Commonwealth were, of course, Albania,

China, and Yugoslavia. Thus, the total number of ruling communist parties—both pro- and anti-Soviet—in the entire World Socialist System stood at 16.

The World Socialist System was regularly juxtaposed against the approximately 82 communist parties external to it, the latter labelled by Soviet writers as the "Revolutionary Movement of the Working Class in Capitalist Countries."[27] Just as in the case of the ruling components of the World Socialist System, this category included parties not subject to Soviet control for want of any viable national pro-Soviet counterpart, e.g., the pro-Chinese parties of Burma, Malaysia, and Thailand and the Eurocommunist-style ones in Mexico, Japan, Italy, Spain, and certain other countries of Western Europe.[28]

The sources consulted for this study did not specifically name the Socialist System and the Revolutionary Movement as subdivisions of the World Communist Movement, but this was their authors' clear implication. Either the World Communist Movement or both the World Socialist System and the Revolutionary Movement of the Working Class in Capitalist Countries were considered, together with the "National Liberation Movement" (see below), to be the major components of the World Revolutionary Process.[29]

Ruling parties were clearly included in the World Communist Movement; the problem was how to classify the non-party institutions of the communist-ruled nations. For our purposes here, they will be considered as part of the World Communist Movement. Taken as a whole, the World Communist Movement was variously described as having "the leading, vanguard role" within the World Revolutionary Process[30] and as being "the most influential political force of our time."[31]

Within this elaborate classification structure, the World Socialist System was regarded by Soviet writers, not surprisingly, as senior in authority and importance to the Revolutionary Movement of the Working Class in Capitalist Countries. Academician M. Mitin makes this plain when he describes the former as "the main bulwark of the World Revolutionary Movement" and the latter as merely "another chief force of the World Revolutionary Process."[32] Besides, Soviet writers habitually ranked the "Socialist System" first and the "Revolutionary Movement" second in their descriptions of the World Communist Movement.[33]

That Russia wanted to be known as supreme within the World Socialist System was evident in statements by spokesmen from the most subservient communist countries, e.g., the Czech Duvan Rovensky's characterization of the CPSU as "this most experienced and steeled formation of the World

Communist Movement. . .the natural leader of the Communist movement throughout the world" and as the unit which "plays the decisive role in the struggle against imperialism and war."[34] Such views, of course, represented only the most pro-Soviet end of the spectrum. Deviations from them caused many stresses and strains within the movement.

The "National Liberation Movement" in "former colonies and semi-colonies" occupied a role secondary to the World Communist Movement in the World Revolutionary Process simply because, as noted above, the struggle between capitalism and socialism was regarded as the "chief contradiction. . .of the contemporary era."[35] G. Shakhnazarov spelled this out when he contrasted the World Communist Movement, "unquestionably the most influential political force of our time," with the National Liberation Movement, "the other most important international force."[36] According to Soviet writers, the national liberation and communist movements were linked together because of their common enemy, "imperialism."[37]

The components of the National Liberation Movement were not neatly identified, but certain ones of them seemed to emerge from the mass of writings on the subject as well as from the patterns of representation at communist party congresses and in communist front organizations. Though communist parties, where present, participated in the National Liberation Movement in Asia, Africa, and Latin America, it was the "revolutionary democratic parties" that were treated by Soviet writers as the *distinctive* progressive elements in this category.[38] Hence, discussions of components of the National Liberation Movement concentrated on Africa and Asia, where such parties were most often found; in Latin America, they were rare.

One authoritative source, Boris Ponomarev, explained the difference. Latin America, in contrast to Africa and non-communist Asia, had "a relatively developed capitalism," a strong and experienced working class, a long history of revolutionary struggle, and communist parties in all countries.[39]

Revolutionary democratic parties usually, but not always, were ruling parties. When they were, they were said to rule "countries of socialist orientation" as the "vanguard of the National Liberation Movement."[40] These countries were said to differ from communist countries in that the former had not yet left the world capitalist system even though the national economy of the majority of them was dominated by the state sector.[41] The revolutionary democratic parties also were different in that they reflected multi-class interests and failed to have a cohesive doctrine and discipline.[42] Though generally regarded by Soviet writers as being dominated by petit bourgeois and other non-working class elements,[43] virtually all revolutionary democratic parties had acquired at least some Marxists by late 1972, according to Soviet Afro-Asian specialist A. Kiva.[44]

According to Soviet writers on the subject, an elite set of these revolutionary democratic parties came closer to being virtual communist parties than did others. These others were the "vanguard (revolutionary democratic) parties," which had stricter class and ideological standards for membership and had openly opted for "scientific socialism," i.e., the Soviet brand of communism.[45] The definitive publication, Soviet-edited *First Hand Information* (Prague: 1988) listed the following as ruling "vanguard" parties at the time:

> People's Democratic Party of Afghanistan (PDPA)
> Popular Movement for the Liberation of Angola-Labor Party (MPLA-PT)
> Party of the People's Revolution of Benin (PPRB)
> Congolese Party of Labor (PCT)
> Workers' Party of Ethiopia (WPE)
> Congress Party for Madagascar Independence (AKFM)— junior partner only
> Mozambique Liberation Front (FRELIMO)
> Sandinist National Liberation Front (FSLN)(Nicaragua)
> Yemen Socialist Party

All of these parties except the PPRB and AKFM addressed a main session of the 26th CPSU Congress (February-March 1981), a privilege granted to only 26 of the 83 regular foreign communist parties present. Later that year, in November, all but the Sandinistas attended the conference on the work of the magazine *Problems of Peace and Socialism*, then the official Soviet-line theoretical monthly of the 63 communist parties[46]; no other revolutionary democratic party attended.

The following are other "vanguard" parties listed in *First Hand Information*. These parties were illegal, small, and generally unimportant in their respective countries.

> National Liberation Front-Bahrain (FLN-B)
> National Democratic Union (UND)(Chad)
> National Democratic Front of South Korea (NDFSK)
> People's Front for the Liberation of Oman (PFLO)

Other parties listed as revolutionary democratic parties by Soviet writers in the 1980s were:[47]

> Algerian National Liberation Front (FLN)
> Burmese Socialist Program Party (BSPP)
> Democratic Party of Guinea (PDG)
> African Party for the Independence of Guinea and the Cape Verde Islands (PAIGC)
> Movement for the Liberation of Sao Tome and Principe (MLSTP)
> Seychelles People's Progressive Front (SPPF)
> Arab Socialist Renaissance (Ba'ath) Party of Syria
> Revolutionary Party of Tanzania (CCM)

The Algerian and Syrian parties were considered important enough to have their representatives address main sessions of the 1981 CPSU Congress (see above). All these parties ran governments, except the Burmese, which was on its way to extinction even at the time it was mentioned in this context.

Unlike the case of the revolutionary democratic parties, other groupings considered authentic parts of the National Liberation Movement seem not to have been listed by Soviet writers. All were in opposition roles in their countries. There are some criteria, however, which enable us to compile a provisional list of neglected organizations that fell into this category. We may call this category "liberation movements proper." These criteria are the kind made by the Czech executive editor of *Problems of Peace and Socialism*, Pavel Auersperg, when he referred to the thirty-eight revolutionary democratic parties and National Liberation Movements attending the East Berlin conference of October 1980.[48]

First, there were some single or unitary organizations of this type that participated in communist-sponsored meetings and constituted the national affiliate of the World Peace Council (WPC) for their respective countries:[49]

> Southwest African People's Organization (SWAPO) (Namibia)
> African National Congress (ANC) (South Africa)
> Popular Front for the Liberation of Saguiel Hamra and Rio de Oro (Frente POLISARIO) (Western Sahara)

Second, we could place at least three united-front groups into the liberation movement proper category. They also participated in communist-sponsored meetings; they all had spokesmen writing in *Problems of Peace and Socialism*, and each included a communist party element.[50]

> Farabundo Marti National Liberation Front (FMLN) (El Salvador)

> Association of Revolutionary Organizations of Guatemala (AROG) or National Revolutionary Unity of Guatemala (URNG)
> Palestine Liberation Organization (PLO)

Adherence to the Soviet line varied among these organizations, with the POLISARIO and PLO perhaps being the least controlled.

There were still other groups on the fringes of the National Liberation Movement participating in both communist-sponsored meetings and in international front organizations. These included the ruling parties of Burundi, Guyana, Iraq, Libya, Madagascar (the dominant party in the ruling coalition), Mali, Sierra Leone, Uganda, Zambia, and Zimbabwe. Of these countries, incidentally, only Guyana, Iraq, and Sierra Leone voted with the United Nations majority condemning Soviet action in Afghanistan in 1980.

Iraq, Mali, and Uganda had been considered revolutionary democracies prior to the downturn in their relations with the USSR. The same had been true of Egypt, Ghana, and Somalia, which, however, appeared no longer to have had any connection with Soviet-line activities by the early 1980s.[51]

Some non-socialist Third World opposition parties participated in communist conferences and fronts. As a group, these appeared more pro-Soviet than the ruling parties just mentioned. These parties included:[52]

> National People's (Awami) Party of Bangladesh
> MAPU Worker-Peasant Party of Chile
> National Progressive-Left Party of Egypt

A third constituent of the Process, less important than either of the other two, was the force of Left-wing Socialism. In February 1974, one Soviet writer listed the Social Democratic Movement, most especially its Left wing, as "one of the influential political currents of our time," meriting a place after the World Communist Movement and the National Liberation Movement.[53] He thus implied that, to some extent, the latter group participated in the World Revolutionary Process, an implication expressed by Boris Ponomarev when discussing socialist-communist cooperation in general during the detente era in 1975.[54]

This statement correlates well with Soviet reports that delegates of "Communist, *left Socialist* [italics mine], and revolutionary democratic parties" attended the 24th CPSU Congress.[55] This observation was also consistent with traditional communist attempts to line up socialist trade unions and youth groups on their side and to recruit individual socialists for communist front organizations. There were two target groups here: far Left socialist parties as such and Left-wingers within more moderate socialist parties.

As an example of far Left socialist parties was a list compiled from attendees at five major international communist conferences between 1978 and 1981. The box score on attendance was as follows:[56]

> New Jewel Movement of Grenada (then ruling) (all 5 conferences)
> Chilean Socialist Party (4)
> Progressive Socialist Party (Lebanon) (3)
> Socialist Party of Japan (2)
> Belgian Socialist Party (2)
> Spanish Socialist Party (2)
> Italian Socialist Party (1)
> People's National Party of Jamaica (1)
> Socialist Revolutionary Party of Peru (1)
> Puerto Rican Socialist Party (1)
> Socialist Party of Uruguay (1)

More commonly, individual Left-wingers from more moderate socialist parties were used in various ways in the communist cause. A good example of this occurred when the World Peace Council (WPC) reorganized itself in late 1980. Socialists from such moderate parties in Australia, Finland, Great Britain, Greece, Norway, Portugal, Senegal, and Switzerland were placed on the Council's Presidential Committee, where they were joined by members of the more radical socialist parties of Chile, Lebanon, and Uruguay.[57]

We summarize this pre-1991 Soviet view of the World Revolutionary Process. The USSR stood at the head of the like-minded communist-ruled states of the Socialist Commonwealth. The latter was, in turn, the core of the World Socialist System, which also included the not-so-like-minded communist-ruled nations. The entire World Socialist System, comprehensively speaking, was considered superior to the Free World's communist parties, e.g., the Revolutionary Movement of the Working Class in Capitalist Countries, which was itself divided into a pro-Soviet majority and a neutralist or anti-Soviet minority.

The totality of all these parties constituted the World Communist Movement, which, in turn, was considered superior to the second great element of the World Revolutionary Process, namely, the National Liberation Movement in Africa, Asia, and Latin America. The latter consisted of largely ruling revolutionary democratic parties, the more developed of which were called "vanguards", and Opposition liberation movements proper.

To all this should be added Left Socialists and others, who constituted a *de facto* third element of the World Revolutionary Process, as illustrated, among other things, by their participation in international communist-front organizations (see below). This complex structure and set of categories was, in fact as well as theory, the organizational vision of the world's communists.

Means of Coordination and Control:
The Conference System and *Problems of Peace and Socialism*
for the World Communist Movement

By the 1970s, Soviet writers were stating that the conference mechanism was the chief means of coordinating the World Communist Movement.[58] Conferences were presumed to permit coordination among parties of equal status, displacing the hierarchical and centralized Moscow domination of Comintern days.[59] Such conferences could be bilateral, regional, or worldwide.

Though it was apparently the bilateral meetings between the CPSU and individual parties that were the scene for whatever direction by the former of the latter took place, it was primarily the worldwide conferences and secondarily the all-European ones that caused the most furor as independent tendencies developed within the movement. Soviet propaganda hearkened back to the three post-World War II world communist party conferences (1957, 1960, 1969) as having laid down the general line for all to follow.[60] Unwillingness to be pressured into following certain aspects of the Soviet line again (especially as regards to China) led to the failure to have another such meeting.[61] Eleven parties that attended the 1960 meeting, including the ruling parties of China, North Korea, North Vietnam, Albania, and Yugoslavia, refused to attend the meeting of 1969. Although these eleven were not expected to attend a subsequent meeting, at least the Eurocommunists and other independents could have been expected to show up. This was not to be. By 1982, the Soviets gave up their attempts to convene another world communist conference.

What the Soviets did accomplish in 1976 was the last full, all-European communist parties conference. By agreeing that no binding party line would be put forth at this meeting and by giving a wide berth to national party autonomy, the Soviets secured the attendance of all the European communists except those of Albania and Iceland. Even the Yugoslavs came.[62]

A previous all-European communist party conference had taken place in 1967. Even though it did no have quite the participation the 1976 meeting did, it was a successful step toward the world meeting that took place two years later. The European communist meeting of 1980, however, had few redeeming features for the Soviets. Billed as a non-controversial peace and disarmament gathering, it was nevertheless boycotted by the independent contingent. These included the "national communists" of the East (Yugoslavia, Romania) as well as the Eurocommunists of the West (Belgium, Great Britain, Italy, the Netherlands, Spain, and Sweden). The boycott was brought on as a protest of the Soviet invasion of Afghanistan.[63]

Party meetings by ruling communist parties suffered a similar decline. All thirteen of the then ruling parties (Cuba had not yet become communist) met just prior to the 1957 world conference to produce the draft of a document to be endorsed by the conference. This document was not signed by the Yugoslavs, however.[64] The subsequent withdrawal of the Chinese and Albanians, the neutrality of the North Koreans and Vietnamese in the Sino-Soviet dispute, and the continued independent posture of Yugoslavia reduced the ruling parties' meetings to representatives from contiguous Warsaw Pact nations, sometimes with the addition of Mongolia and Cuba and, during the 1980s, Laos and Vietnam.

The abortive Soviet campaign, apparently inspired by a July 1973 Warsaw Pact summit, to promote another world communist conference spawned a whole series of smaller regional communist parties meetings.[65] Between July 1973 and September 1981, there were eleven meetings of from four to ten Arab communist parties, four of the four main Scandinavian parties, three of the West European parties, and one each for the La Plata Basin; Mexico, Central America, and Panama; all of Latin America; the Caribbean countries; tropical and southern Africa; Greece, Turkey, and Cyprus; the Persian Gulf and Arabian Peninsula; Canada, Mexico, and the United States; and the Eastern Mediterranean, Middle East, and Red Sea nations.[66]

As it was becoming clear that the Soviets could not achieve a world conference, world-scale meetings of communist parties began to be brought off successfully under the sponsorship of the magazine *Problems of Peace and Socialism* (*World Marxist Review*). In 1978, the magazine and the Bulgarian Communist Party co-sponsored a conference on the "Construction of Socialism and Communism and World Development" in Sofia. Among the 69 communist and four "vanguard" parties attending were 25 of the 29 that had attended the 1976 European communist parties meeting; only Norway, San Marino, Sweden, and Yugoslavia refrained from attending. Even Vietnam, which had not attended the 1969 world conference of 75 communist parties, attended.

This meeting was followed by an October 1980 conference on the "Joint Struggle of the Working Class and National Liberation Movements Against Imperialism, for Social Progress," co-sponsored in East Berlin by the magazine and the East German Socialist Unity Party. The 73 communist parties attending exceeded the number at the 1969 world conference and included seven of the eight parties that boycotted the European communist parties conference just six months earlier. The Yugoslavs stayed away. This latter conference was not limited to communists. Its 38 other units of the World Revolutionary Process helped to identify many of the revolutionary democrats, National Liberation Movement members, and Left socialists described above.

The three international conferences in 1981, 1984, and 1988, devoted to the work of *Problems of Peace and Socialism*, were closely connected to Soviet efforts to hold another world communist parties meeting. At the very first of the three conferences, attended by 82 pro-Soviet and neutralist parties and eight "vanguard" parties, the agenda was expanded to include world issues. The Czech delegate, apparently on behalf of the Soviet Union, proposed the holding of a regular world communist parties conference in the future.[67] There appears to have been a notable lack of response to this suggestion. The Soviet effort may well have ended at this point. In any case, the Russians had to be satisfied with two additional conferences dealing with the work of the magazine.

The 1984 and 1988 meetings also had "vanguard" parties in attendance. Their acceptance by the movement was warm. Consequently, when *Problems of Peace and Socialism* catalogued the world's communist parties in the *First Hand Information* booklet (1988), it included the "vanguards" as well.

The magazine's efforts in the conference sphere was logical in view of the fact that, since its 1958 inception, it had been the only permanent institutional symbol of unity for the world's pro-Moscow and independent communist parties. During its lifetime, the parties' representation on the magazine's staff had gone from 20 to 68 communist parties, plus one for the "vanguards."

The Soviets always seemed in control. The chief editor was always Soviet. Its commission secretaries and department heads all appear to have been Soviet.[68] The magazine had traditionally not carried articles offensive to the Russians in spite of the fact that somewhat independent communists from Italy, Japan, Great Britain, Sweden, Romania, and Spain sat on its editorial council. Individual parties, however, were allowed to delete articles distasteful to them from their own national editions.[69] The Chinese had withdrawn from participation in 1963.

During the last few month's prior to its demise in May 1990, the magazine engaged in an uncharacteristic amount of pluralist thought. This may merely have reflected the "new thinking" in the Soviet Union at the time. Such was the complaint, in fact, of a spokesman for the ever-contentious Japanese Communist Party.[70] In any case, a Soviet defector who had been formerly employed by *Problems* revealed in 1989 that the magazine had been operated by the International Department of the CPSU,[71] thus making it just as much of a front organization, perhaps of a different kind, as those discussed below.

Means of Coordination and Control:
The International Communist Front Organizations
for the World Revolutionary Process

Though other elements of the World Revolutionary Process, like the communists and the "vanguards", did participate in a limited way in the conference system, it was the front organizations—both international and national—that provided the chief means of coordination here. In fact, this appeared to be the main function of the fronts. Participation in them by and large defined which groups were members of the World Revolutionary Process. At the international level, the fronts had (and still have) a policy formation structure--bureau, presidential committee, council, congress, or their equivalent--which met periodically. There was also a permanent secretariat at its headquarters charged with carrying out policies on a day-to-day basis.

Soviet control at this permanent, day-to-day level was usually exercised through a Soviet member of the secretariat, while at the policy level there was the almost inevitable Soviet vice president.[72] Evidence of Soviet control was manifested in a negative way by the withdrawal of many socialist and other non-communist groups, plus the Yugoslavs, from the fronts following the 1947 onset of the Cold War and the 1948 break with Tito, respectively.

Other evidence included the gradual cessation of Chinese and Albanian activity in the secretariat as the Sino-Soviet split widened in the early 1960s. Thereafter came the elimination of Frenchmen and Italians from top leadership positions in the trade union, youth, and women's fronts following the criticism of the 1968 invasion of Czechoslovakia by their respective communist parties.

There was also the overall, continuous support of Soviet foreign policy that led to self-criticism on this issue during 1989-1990 by *Soviet* officials from within at least the two major international fronts, the World Peace Council (WPC) and World Federation of Trade Unions (WFTU).[73] It fell to the Iraqi secretary general of the Afro-Asian Peoples' Solidarity Organization (AAPSO) to link these criticisms with the changes brought about by Gorbachev[74]—evidence that Soviet control continued even during the criticism of it!

The primacy of the WPC among the international fronts could be seen in the claims of communist writers that the peace movement was the most important "joint action" of the "anti-imperialist forces" and the most important of the movements "based on common specific objectives of professional interests,"[75] i.e., the international communist front organizations.

WPC was undoubtedly the largest of all the fronts. Although total membership figures have never been published, it declared that it had membership in about 145 countries, more than any other front.[76] Nor did it have the occupational, age, gender, or regional requirements of the others.

Finally, WPC was the one front that helped coordinate the others by giving their representatives positions on its leadership organs. For example, on the slate of WPC officers elected in 1983, two of its 38 vice presidencies were reserved for the secretary general of the WFTU and the president of the Women's International Democratic Federation (WIDF), the two largest fronts for which membership statistics are available. Among the additional 179 members of the WPC's presidential committee were 18 representatives from the WFTU, the WIDF, and 13 other fronts. Top leaders of still other international fronts could be found in the country delegations to the 1500-plus Council of the WPC.[77] Thus were included almost all the important leaders of the 18 "closely coordinating non-governmental organizations," as they called themselves, that were ever noted as meeting together at least ten times during the 1979-89 period in what was yet another coordination process.

The trade union movement, especially as embodied in the WFTU, was mentioned by at least one Soviet writer as the second most important area of front activity.[78] The trade unions were especially successful in binding together European, Asian, and Latin American communists with Arab and African revolutionary democrats. They were much less successful than the

WPC in holding on to socialists. Most of WFTU socialist affiliates, in fact, withdrew during the 1947-49 period. In 1978, the Eurocommunist Italian General Confederation of Labor did so as well.

The WFTU extended its influence by spawning worldwide occupational specialty organizations called Trade Unions International (TUI's) and by joining with regional confederations in Latin America, Africa, and the Arab World through joint affiliation with national affiliates. In the latter two regions, this involved the only regional confederations extant, namely, the official trade union organizations of the Organization of African Unity (OAU) and the Arab League. It is noteworthy that, as of 1983, all three of these regional trade union confederations had slots on WPC's Council.[79]

Probably next in order of importance, though not in size (the WIDF was that), was the World Federation of Democratic Youth (WFDY). Though subject to the same sort of non-communist withdrawals in its early years as the WFTU, WFDY took pride in retaining the youth organizations of the left-wing Socialist Parties of Chile and Japan, along with their communist counterparts. Together with its much smaller student organization, the International Union of Students (IUS), the WFDY co-sponsored the World Youth Festivals, thirteen of which, between 1947 and 1989, constituted the most highly attended series of regularly recurring front meetings ever—between 17,000 and 34,000 persons.[80]

Aside from the WFTU, the WIDF, and the WFDY, the only other international fronts with their two top leaders on the WPC Presidential Committee as of 1983 were the Afro-Asian Peoples' Solidarity Committee (AAPSO) and the Asian Bhuddists Conference for Peace (ABCP). These two geographically bounded organizations were founded in 1957 and 1970, respectively, after the first successes of the fronts described above (1945-1950).

The AAPSO was at least partially a Soviet reaction to having been excluded from the 1955 Bandung Conference and the Non-Aligned Movement (NAM) that followed from it. This organization was an apparent outgrowth of the Soviet-dominated WPC. Thus, it came as no surprise that the same Indian national affiliate served both international organizations; Burhan Shahidi had been the vice president of both China's peace and Afro-Asian affiliates; and the Iraqi Aziz Sherif had been a vice president of both the internationals.

The Chinese seemed to have been a real force in the organization until it became evident in 1967 that, because of Soviet objection, they could not have the organization's next conference in Beijing. A Soviet defector explained that the CPSU International Department had claimed control of the AAPSO by the mid-1960s, thus explaining the Chinese failure to be able to host the organization's conference. In any case, the Chinese withdrew from active participation.[81]

The Egyptians furnished the headquarters site and much of the staffing, but never seem to have recovered from the 1978 assassination of their Yusuf al-Sibai, AAPSO secretary general and perhaps the dominant personality in the organization. Throughout, the Soviet role was masked enough so that AAPSO appeared to have succeeded in its purpose of enlisting a wider circle of supporters than participated in the other fronts. Its Egyptian president, Murad Ghalib, and Cypriot vice president, Vassos Lyssarides, were outstanding in accomplishing this objective.

Aside from the four major fronts, the WFTU, WIDF, WFDY, AAPSO, and the relatively minor ABCP, each having two leaders on the WPC Presidential Committee, there were twelve others important enough to be included in the meetings of the "closely cooperating non-governmental organizations." (Sometimes *Problems of Peace and Socialism* was represented as well.) The twelve were:

> Berlin Conference of European Catholics (BCEC)
> Christian Peace Conference (CPC)
> Continental Organization of Latin American Students (OCLAE)
> International Association of Democratic Lawyers (IADL)
> International Federation of Resistance Movements (FIR)
> International Institute for Peace (IIP)
> International Organization of Journalists (IOJ)
> International Radio and Television Organization (OIRT)
> International Union of Students (IUS)
> Organization of Solidarity of the Peoples of Africa, Asia, and Latin America (OSPAAAL)
> World Federation of Scientific Workers (WFSW)
> World Federation of Teachers' Unions (FISE)

Of these twelve, the BCEC, CPC, IIP, IOJ, IUS, and OSPAAAL had one position each on the WPC Presidential Committee and the IADL a position on the WPC Council. The president of the FISE was included in the Sri Lankan contingent of the WPC's Council (all as of 1983-86).[82]

The fact that these fronts united communists, revolutionary democrats, other National Liberation Movement members, Left Socialists, and others to promote Soviet foreign policy interests was not entirely lost on the politically more sophisticated. Many governments not particularly pro-Soviet endorsed their nationals' participation in such groups as AAPSO or the Arab and African regional trade unions related to both the WPC and

WFTU because they saw actual or potential political, economic, and/or military benefits coming from a close relationship with the Soviets. Besides, many, no doubt, had the "gut reaction" that anything anti-Western could not be all bad; the Soviet anti-imperialism propaganda did strike responsive cords, even among non-Leftists. The fact that the U.N. pretended to take the nonpartisan attestations of these organizations at face value in granting the bulk of them official nongovernmental status for advisory purposes fit in perfectly with the gradual envelopment of that body by ever-multiplying numbers of Third World members.

Ultimate Means of Coordination and Control: The Foreign Affairs Departments of the CPSU

As mentioned above, the post-World War II era saw a CPSU International Department dealing with Free World communist parties and whatever non-communist parties and liberation movements that may have had dealings with the CPSU. Department members were included in CPSU delegations abroad and hosted foreign delegations to the Soviet Union; some were even stationed in Soviet embassies overseas.[83] What information we have on the subject indicates that a developed capitalist country generally warranted a full-time staffer, no matter what its size or what the importance of its party, whereas Third World nations were grouped by two's or three's for one person to handle (unless the country was very large, like India).[84] Similarly, CPSU archives reveal that the top communist party recipients of Soviet funding during 1987-1990 were, in order, those of France, the U.S., Finland, Portugal, and Greece,[85] all of developed nations, but not Eurocommunist. At one time at least, West Germany was known to have had two specialists, while Japan had its own "sector" throughout. Finally, the two short term chiefs of the Department, following the long tenure of Boris Ponomarev, Anatoliy Dobrynin (1986-1988), and Valentin Falin (1988-1991?), had been ambassadors to the U.S. and West Germany, respectively.

The fact that two important front organizations, the WFTU and the AAPSO, were known to have been handled by the same Department staffer,[86] a pattern presumably replicated for other similar bodies, is not surprising when one realizes that each Soviet affiliate of an international front had its *own* International Department, which presumably helped out in the control effort as well as in masking it.

While on the subject of other International Departments, we should note that each of the communist and other parties with which the CPSU dealt apparently had one (or an equivalent) to take up its end of the relationship. The CPSU Department for Relations with the Communist Parties of the Socialist Countries was incorporated back into the International Department from which it came in the 1988 year of retrenchment, with its former chief, Rafel Fedorov, joining the former International Department deputy Karen Brutents as one of two first deputies of the newly consolidated department.

Elements Outside the System

Certain Leftist groups apparently, to a greater or lesser degree, remained outside the World Revolutionary Process from the Soviet standpoint. The Trotskyists, generally willing to put world (and their own national) revolution above Soviet foreign policy interests, were therefore traditionally regarded as "Left adventurists." However, they had long received support from the Soviet-recognized Cubans at the international level and are currently showing a new-found vitality and flexibility. The Pol Pot-Khmer Rouge element in Cambodia, likewise too far Left to be inside the Soviet pale, has, it appears, received support from Soviet-recognized China off and on; it is still a factor in its country.

The Communist Party of the Philippines and its New People's Army and other fronts were long ignored in Soviet writings; they at least received a footnote in *First Hand Information* (1988) and are now recognized by most other communist forces as the chief representatives of the Philippine Left abroad. This is in lieu of the Philippine Communist Party which the Soviets have traditionally recognized.

The now nearly defunct Peruvian Sendoro Luminoso was another extreme and active Leftist revolutionary group which the Soviets apparently found "inconvenient" to their foreign policy interests.

This brief survey of the background of the communist theories of political organization, the Comintern, and the Soviet-controlled affiliations and front organizations does not pretend to be comprehensive or complete. It does, however, give us insight into the former Soviet Union's intricate web of organizational relationships and its ability to mask them in order to give an impression of widespread inclusiveness and support. We now turn to the contemporary network of communist connections and organizational strategies.

Notes

1. Most of this chapter is based on the author's "The Communist Movement and Its Allies" in Ralph M. Goldman (ed.), *Transnational Parties* (Lanham, MD: University Press of America, 1983), ch. 2.

2. Witold S. Sworakowski (ed.), *World Communism: A Handbook, 1918-1965* (Stanford: Hoover Institution. 1973) (hereafter referred to as *Handbook*), p. 80; R. Palme Dutt, *The Internationale* (London: Lawrence and Wishart, 1964), p. 156.

3. Milorad M. Drachkovitch and Branko Lazitch (eds.), *The Comintern: Historical Highlights* (New York: Praeger, 1966), p. 54.

4. *Handbook*, pp. 84-85.

5. Ibid., pp. 83-85.

6. Ibid., p. 88; Ralph M. Goldman, op. cit., Appendix C.

7. Leonard Schapiro, "The International Department of the CPSU: Key to Soviet Policy," *International Journal* (Toronto), vol. XXXII, Winter 1966-7, no. 1, pp. 42,44.

8. Ibid., p. 43.

9. See Drachkovitch and Lazitch, op. cit., pp. 45-54.

10. *Handbook*, pp. 88-89.

11. Ibid., pp. 80-88; Ralph M. Goldman, op. cit., pp. 39-40.

12. *Handbook*, p. 78.

13. Ibid., p. 88.

14. Ibid., p. 77.

15. Ibid., p. 210.

16. Ibid., pp. 210-211.

17. K. Maydanik and G. Mirskiy, "The National Liberation Struggle: the Current Stage," *Mirovaya Ekonomika i Mexhdunrodnyye Otnosheniya* (Moscow), no. 6, June 1991, p. 18 (trans.: Joint Publications Research Service, no. 78972); N. N. Inozemtsev, "A Revolutionary Step for Millions," *Knizhnoye Obozrenie* (Moscow), no. 3, February 20, 1981, p. 11 (trans.: Joint Publications Research Service, no. 77897); V. V. Zagladin (ed.), *The International Communist Movement: Sketch of Strategy and Tactics*, p. 4 (trans.: Joint

Publications Research Service, no. 57044); M. Mitin, "A Doctrine Which Is Transforming the World," *Izvestia* (Moscow), April 20, 1974 (trans.: Foreign Broadcast Information Service, May 8, 1974, Supplement.

18. Ibid.; V. V. Zagladin, op. cit., p. 4.

19. V. V. Zagladin, "A Few Problems of the Communist Movement and the Policy of the CPSU," *Neues Deutschland* (East Berlin), May 4, 1972.

20. B. Ponomarev, "V. I. Lenin and the International Communist Movement," *Kommunist* (Moscow, no. 2, February 1974, p. 4 (trans.: Joint Publications Research Service, no. 61497); B. Ponomarev, Lenin Anniversary Meeting speech, Radio Moscow, April 22, 1974 (trans.: Foreign Broadcast Information Service, April 23, 1974); V. V. Zagladin, "A New Historical Stage," *Problems of History* (Moscow), no. 6, June 1974, p. 1 (trans.: Joint Publications Research Service, no. 64951).

21. Boris Vesnin, "The Communists and Peace, Detente, Disarmament," *New Times* (Moscow), no. 49, 1981, p. 10; New China News Agency (Peiping), July 1, 1981, as quoted in Richard F. Staar (ed.), *1982 Yearbook on International Communist Affairs* (Stanford, CA: Hoover Institution, 1982), p. 174.

22. Alexander Subbotin (ed.), *First Hand Information* (Prague: Peace and Socialism, 1988), pp. 9, 67.

23. Ibid., p. 9; Boris Vesnin, op. cit., p. 10; "Brezhnev Report to 26th CPSU Congress," Radio Moscow, February 23, 1981 (trans: Foreign Broadcast Information Service, February 24, 1981, Supplement).

24. Alexander Subbotin, op. cit., pp. 51-53, 72-74, and 138-40.

25. M. Mitin, op. cit, pp. 1, 4; V. V. Zagladin (ed.), *The International Communist Movement*, op. cit., p. 47.

26. "Brezhnev Report to 26th CPSU Congress," op. cit.

27. V. V. Zagladin (ed.), *The International Communist Movement*, op. cit., p. 59; M. Mitin, op. cit., p. 4; Ye. Kuskov, "The Most Active and Influential Force," *Kommunist* (Moscow), no. 17, November 1972, p. 107 (trans.: Joint Publications Research Service, no. 57988); N.N. Inozmetsev, op. cit., p. 11.

28. See Ralph M. Goldman, op. cit., Appendix A.

29. G. Shakhnazarov, "On the Problem of Correlation of Forces in the World," *Kommunist* (Moscow), no. 3, February 1974, p. 100 (trans.: Joint Publications Research Service, no. 61776); M. Mitin, op. cit., p. 4.

30. V. V. Zagladin (ed.), *The International Communist Movement*, op. cit., p. 4.

31. G. Shakhnazarov, op. cit., p. 100.

32. M. Mitin, op. cit., p. 4.

33. Ibid.; V. V. Zagladin (ed.), *The International Communist Movement*, op. cit., p. 47; Ye. Kuskov, op. cit., pp. 97, 99-100.

34. Dusan Rovensky, "The Development of Cooperation Among the Communist and Workers' Parties," *Rude Pravo* (Prague), 31 May 31, 1974, p. 3 (trans.: Joint Publications Research Service, no. 62290); Konstantin Tellalov, "Under the Banner of the Struggle for Peace, Democracy, and Socialism," *Rabotnichesko Delo* (Sofia), June 5, 1974 (trans.: Foreign Broadcast Information Service, June 7, 1974).

35. V. V. Zagladin (ed.), *The International Communist Movement*, op. cit., pp. 66-67.

36. G. Shakhnazarov, op. cit., p. 100.

37. V. V. Zagladin (ed.), *The International Communist Movement*, op. cit., p. 66.

38. Ibid., pp. 199-205; V. G. Solodovnikov, A. B. Letnev, and P. I. Manchkha, *Political Parties of Africa* (Moscow), pp. 169-170 (trans.: Joint Publications Research Service, no. 52950).

39. B. Ponomarev, "Topical Problems in the Theory of the World Revolutionary Process," *Kommunist* (Moscow), no. 15, October 1971, pp. 70, 75 (trans.: Joint Publications Research Service, no. 54571).

40. R. A. Ulyanovskiy, "Great October and Revolutionary Process in Asian and African Countries," *Problems of the Far East* (Moscow), no. 2, 1977, p. 15 (trans.: Joint Publications Research Service, no. 69699).

41. A. Kiva, "Sotsialisticheskaya orientatsiya, Nekotorie problemy teorii i praktiki," *Mirovaya ekonomika i mezhdunarodnyye otnosheniya* (Moscow), no. 10, October 1976, p. 23.

42. A. Kiva, "Countries of Socialist Orientation: Some Aspects of Their Political Development," *International Affairs* (Moscow), October 1973, p. 32; V. V. Zagladin (ed.), *The International Communist Movement*, op. cit., p. 255; V. G. Solodovnikov et al., op. cit., p. 75; G.

Shakhnazarov, op. cit., p. 100.

43. A. Belskiy, "The National Liberation Movement: Laws and Prospects," *Asia and Africa Today* (Moscow), no. 3, 1975, p. 45 (trans.: Joint Publications Research Service, no. 64667); V. V. Zagladin, *The International Communist Movement*, op. cit., pp. 79, 206; A. Kiva, "Countries of Socialist Orientation...," op. cit., pp. 33, 35-36.

44. Ibid., p. 37.

45. Veniamin Chirkin, (article unstated), *Asia and Africa Today* (Moscow), no. 4, July-August 1981, pp. 4-5 (trans.: Joint Publications Research Service, no. 79176); Vi. Li, "Social Revolution in Afro-Asian Countries and Scientific Socialism," *Aziya i Afrika Segodnya* (Moscow), no. 3, March 1981, p. 12 (trans.: Joint Publications Research Service, no. 78507).

46. "Communique," *World Marxist Review* (Toronto, December 1981), p. 1.

47. Veniamin Chirkin, op. cit., pp. 4-8; Nikolay Dmitriyevich Kosukhin, "Development Trends of the Countries of Socialist Orientation," *Rabochiy Kiass i Sovremenny Mir* (Moscow), no. 4, July-August 1981, p. 65 (trans.: Joint Publications Research Service, no. 79561).

48. Pavel Auersperg, "International Meeting of the Forces of World Progress," *Tribuna* (Prague),'no. 48, November 26, 1980, p. 12 (trans.: Joint Publications Research Service, no. 77193).

49. World Peace Council, *List of Members, 1980-1983* (Helsinki), pp. 9, 97, 105, 128, and 155. That this was the situation in Bahrain is inferred from the fact that no mention was made of a Bahrain Peace Committee in the listing of World Peace Council members from that country (p. 10).

50. Norman F. Howard, "Jordan," in Richard F. Staar (ed.), *1975 Yearbook of International Communist Affairs*, op. cit., p. 592; *Granma* (Havana), December 28, 1975; Thomas P. Anderson, "El Salvador," and Daniel L. Primo, "Guatemala," in Richard F. Staar (ed.), *1981 Yearbook of International Communist Affairs*, op. cit., pp. 72, 76.

51. Five of these countries were specifically stated to have dropped from this category, but Iraq merely ceased to be mentioned in the 1981 listings. R. Ulyanovskiy (article unstated), *Kommunist* (Moscow) no. 11, July 1979, p. 132 (trans.: Joint Publications Research Service, no.

74317) A. Kiva, "Countries of Socialist Orientation...," op. cit., p. 37.

52. See Ralph M. Goldman, op. cit., Appendix A.

53. G. Shakhnazarov, op. cit., p. 100.

54. B. Ponomarev, "Topical Problems in the Theory of the World Revolutionary Process," op. cit., p. 72. See also, *Pravda* (Moscow), April 12, 1983 (trans.: Foreign Broadcast Information Service, April 13, 1992) for social democratic participation in communist-sponsored East Berlin Karl Marx conference.

55. Vitaliy Korionov commentary, Radio Moscow, June 5, 1972 (trans.: Foreign Broadcast Information Service, June 7, 1972).

56. See Ralph M. Goldman, op. cit., Appendix A.

57. *New Perspectives* (Helsinki), no. 3, 1981, p. 2.

58. V. V. Zagladin (ed.), *The International Communist Movement*, op. cit., p. 332; Ye. Kuskov, op. cit., p. 95.

59. "Task at the Present Stage of the Struggle Against Imperialism and United Action of the Communist and Workers' Parties and All Anti-Imperialist Forces," *World Marxist Review Information Bulletin* (Toronto), no. 12, 1969, p. 63; Ye. Kuskov, op. cit., pp. 93-94.

60. V. V. Zagladin (ed.), *The International Communist Movement*, op. cit., p. 333; Ye. Kuskov, op. cit., p. 95.

61. *Christian Science Monitor* (Boston), June 30, 1975; *Guardian* (Manchester), April 9, 1974 . Aside from the dent it would put in their "triumphalist" proclamations, it was the sensitivity to the China issue on the part of the more independent communist parties that probably kept the Soviets from formally reading the Chinese out of the movement. An Australian communist leader noted in this connection that no one had proposed the excommunication of China at the 28-party European communist preliminary conference of October 1974. Edwin Scharf in *Volkstimme* of October 22, 1974).

62. Richard F. Staar (ed.), *1977 Yearbook on International Communist Affairs*, op. cit., pp. xi, and Milorad M. Drakovitch, "Conference of Communist and Workers' Parties in Europe," ibid., pp. 572-573.

63. Richard F. Staar (ed.), *1981 Yearbook of International Communist Affairs*, op. cit., p. xxxiii.

64. Robert M. McNeal (ed.), *International Relations Among Communists* (Englewood Cliffs, NJ: Prentice-Hall, 1967), p. 16.

65. See the author's "The Communist Movement and Its Allies," op. cit., pp. 41-42.

66. Ibid.

67. *Pravda* (Moscow), November 27, 1981 (trans: Foreign Broadcast Information Services, December 8, 1981).

68. *World Marxist Review* (Toronto), July 1973, p. 114; October 1974, p. 50; January 1975, p. 137.

69. See the author's "The Communist Movement and Its Allies," op. cit., p. 43.

70. See the author's "International Communist Organizations," in Richard F. Staar (ed.), *1991 Yearbook on International Communist Affairs*, op. cit., p. 436.

71. *Washington Times*, May 3, 1989.

72. See the author's "International Communist Organizations" in Richard F. Staar (ed.), *1984 Yearbook on International Communist Affairs*, op. cit., pp. 428-434; and *1990...*, op. cit., p. 500.

73. Ibid., *1990...* , p. 502; *1991...*, p. 445.

74. Ibid.

75. G. Shakhnazarov, op. cit., p. 101; Ye. Kuskov, op. cit., p. 103.

76. See the author's "International Communist Organizations" in Richard F. Staar (ed.), *1991 Yearbook on International Communist Affairs*, op. cit., p. 438.

77. World Peace Council, op. cit.

78. G. Shakhnazarov, op. cit., p. 101. At least one non-communist writer agrees with this placement. (W.J. Vogt, *The International Front Organizations of Communism* [Johannesburg: by the author, 1960], p. 3).

79. World Peace Council, op. cit., pp. 167-168.

80. Clive Rose, *The Soviet Propaganda Network* (London: Pinter Publishers, 1988), p. 131.

81. Ibid., p. 81.

82. World Peace Council, op. cit., pp. 144, 165-168.

83. Robert W. Kitrinos,"International Department of the CPSU," *Problems of Communism* (Washington, D.C.)., September-October 1984, pp. 74-75.

84. See author's supplement to Robert W. Kitrinos, op. cit., pp. 68-73.

85. "Moscow Gold," *Political Warfare* (Washington, D.C.), Spring 1992, p. 13.

86. See author's supplement to Robert W. Kitrinos, op. cit., p. 73.

Chapter 2

The North Koreans
As Ideological Leaders

Claims to Leadership

The Korean Workers' Party (KWP) newspaper *Nodong Sinmun* carried an article on March 31, 1995, declaring that the Democratic People's Republic of Korea (DPRK) was an "ideological superpower." It went on to say that ideology was the most important element of power: "an ideological superpower is the most powerful country. . .ideology is stronger than steel. . .ideology decides all things." The DPRK's "chuche" ideology (an allegedly home-grown variety of "self-help" Stalinism) is described as "the guiding thought of our time, which occupies the most eminent place in the history of human thought." Its development is attributed solely to the late Kim Il-song and to his son and successor, Kim Chong-il: "our guiding ideology is great because our leader. . .is great."

This claim has been taken up by North Korean apologists the world over, whose statements have been dutifully replayed by the DPRK media. Kim Il-song was described as "the most distinguished thinker and theoretician of our era" by T. B. Mukherjee, president of the Asian Regional Institute of the Chuche Idea, and as "the only leader who founded the most correct guiding idea" (sic) by Keshar Jung Rayamaj, chairman of the Nepal Democratic Socialist Party.[1] As for Kim Chong-il:

"He has performed immortal feats which could not be done by any other thinker, philosopher, and practitioner. . . . He is the supreme incarnation of ethics and morality and creator of communist virtues," according to Chairman Pekka Rantala of the Finnish National Committee for the Study of the Chuche Idea.[2] "He is the most outstanding great man among the leaders of the world for his great idea," according to Cambodia's King Norodom Sihanouk.[3]

With such a great ideology and such great leadership, it would seem logical for the DPRK and its ruling KWP to be called upon to exercise a dominant role internationally. Such calls have indeed been made by foreigners and have been played up by the North Korean media. On March 14, 1994, the *Pyongyang Times*, the official English-language organ, noted that Keith Bennett, political editor of the *Asian Times* (London), had written a book entitled *Korea: Pioneer of Communism* in which he stated that Kim Il-song and his KWP were alone capable of leading the international communist movement, that is, collectively, the communist and related parties of the world. In late 1995, the leaders of two of Russia's smaller communist parties would express similar views regarding Kim Il-song's successor. Russian Communist Workers' Party (RCWP) Chairman Viktor Anpilov stated in October that "the center of unity of the world's communists at present is Comrade Kim Chong-il."[4] The following month Union of Communist Parties-Communist Party of the Soviet Union (UCP-CPSU) Chairman Oleg Shenin said that "the Workers' Party of Korea plays the leading role in the struggle for socialism [read communism] in the world at present, and Comrade Kim Chong-il is the supreme commander of the struggle."[5]

Many, in fact, see KWP leadership extending beyond the narrow confines of the communist party complex to encompass the entire World Revolutionary Process, that is, in Soviet parlance, communists, like-minded Left-wing revolutionary democrats, socialists, liberation movement members, and even independents.[6] Justice Party Chairman Johann Fruehewirth (Austria) stated in February 1995: "I believe only his excellency Kim Chong-il. . .can lead the world revolutionary process *and* [italics mine] the international communist movement."[7] Similarly, Secretary General of the October 8th Revolutionary Movement (MR-8) Claudio Campos (Brazil) noted in September of that year that Kim Chong-il "is the destiny of humankind and the great leader of the world revolution."[8] Earlier, in August 1955, Chairman of the National Congress Party Norand Achakeso (Ghana) may have gone even further when he stated that "the Workers' Party of Korea has become the *only* [italics mine] beacon of hope for progressive mankind."[9] Finally, the KWP's own *Nodong Samhun* on May 16, 1995, seemed to have gone as far as possible in implying Pyongyang's leadership potential for the Non-Aligned Movement (of which the DPRK is, ironically, a member) along with "all other anti-imperialist, independent forces of the world."

The Pyongyang Declaration and Its Supporters

The attempt to exercise such wide-ranging leadership could be seen in the promulgation of the strident and extremist document, "Let Us Defend and Advance the Socialist Cause" (Pyongyang Declaration, Appendix I), in April, 1992, on the occasion of Kim Il-song's 80th birthday and the attempts to secure adherence to it ever since. Representatives of 70 of the political parties in Pyongyang for the 80th birthday celebrations were initial signatories to the document. By early 1997, an additional 165 groups had adhered to it. Most were inconsequential extremist organizations, however, and they included only 38 of the 119 parties listed in the authoritative *First Hand Information* as communist or "vanguard" parties. The latter, published in 1988 and compiled by *World Marxist Review* chief editor Alexander Subbotin, became the definitive listing of those groups recognized by the Soviet Union at that time. Even the figure 38 is stretching a point since, by including the main successors of the original 119, we have counted four derivative organizations of the once unified Communist Party of the Soviet Union (CPSU).

At least three aspects of the Pyongyang Declaration might be noted here. First, its tone appears more moral than materialistic. "Socialism's" alleged superiority is couched in terms of equality,"true democracy," and even human rights rather than economic efficiency. Likewise, "reactionary" capitalism and "imperialist" "neo-colonialism" are faulted for promoting inequality and exploitation, not for any lack of productivity. In other words, it is the division of the pie, not its size, that is in question here. Second, the Declaration criticizes the erstwhile regimes of the Soviet Union and Eastern Europe. Specifically, they are chided for failure "to build a social structure conforming to the fundamental requirements of the popular masses and build socialism suited to the demands of scientific socialism." As to the former, it is stated that "the popular masses [should] become the genuine masters of society" ("true democracy"?—see above); and as to the latter, the revolutionary movement in each country should: (1) be independent and tailored to local conditions (a slap at erstwhile Soviet domination?), but at the same time (2) "not abandon its revolutionary principles at any time [or] under any circumstances" (a slap at Gorbachevian-type reforms?). Third, there is here the traditionally Marxist tension between proclaiming the inevitable victory of "socialism" and the almost frantic call for international solidarity, for individual national revolutionary parties to work together in order to bring this victory about.

In the Former Soviet Union

The former Soviet Union is one of the areas of North Korean success. The major communist parties of contiguous Russia, Ukraine, and Belarus all signed the Pyongyang Declaration. They are all important, maintaining pluralities in their respective legislatures, but not necessarily controlling their governments. In light of their signatures, they seem to be reformed only to the extent that they are compelled to operate in pluralistic political systems and market-oriented economies, which presumably makes them more like traditional *West* European communist parties. The refusal of these three parties to drop the word "communist" from their titles and statements by some of their spokesmen only emphasize their closeness to the North Koreans. When the extremely anti-capitalist, anti-imperialist content of the Pyongyang Declaration signed by them is added, it all more than suggests their lack of reformation, particularly when compared to their East European counterparts. The latter, by and large. dropped the term "communist" from their titles and did not sign the Declaration.

Gennady Zyuganov, chairman of the dominant Communist Party-Russian Federation (CP-RF), told a visiting KWP delegation to Moscow in January 1995 that the Korean experience in "party building" (one of Kim Chong-il's pet subjects) constituted a "valuable example" and that the two parties should strengthen their relationship.[10] And in April 1997 the only non-ruling communist party delegations to the CP-RF's 4th Congress highlighted by the host party's newspaper represented Pyongyang Declaration signatories (in Cyprus, India [CPI-M], Lebanon, and the Ukraine).[11] It was at this meeting that the CP-RF made its first open claim to be the successor to the Communist Party of the Soviet Union.[12]

While one small group to the Right of the CP-RF, the Russian Socialist Workers Party, also signed the Pyongyang Declaration, those on its Left seemed to be closest of all to the North Koreans. This reinforces the contention that the North Koreans are generally a Leftist influence, even within the communist movement. The All-Union Communist Party of Bolsheviks (AUCPB) and the Russian Communist Workers Party (RCWP) were described by the extremely pro-KWP *The New Worker* (London) of May 27, 1994, as "the two main Marxist-Leninist organizations in Russia today." They were the only two Russian groups to attend the European "chuche" seminar held in Copenhagen in February 1995. Unlike the CP-RF and RCWP, they failed to participate in the conferences sponsored by the French Communist Party (PCF) during 1990-96. These are additional indicators of extremism (see below.)

In November 1994, AUCPB Secretary General Nina Andreyeva called the Pyongyang Declaration "the first collective answer to the maneuvers of modern world imperialism."[13] RCWP Chairman Anpilov's later paean to Kim Chong-il has already been noted. After Oleg Shenin had apparently been ousted from the CP-RF leadership at the latter's January 1995 Congress, his UCP-CPSU signed the Pyongyang Declaration and he, too, started to make enthusiastic statements regarding Kim Chong-il and the KWP again, as noted above.

The Declaration-signing Communist Party of Belarus (CPB) appears to be about the same as the CP-RF. It participates in the PCF conference system and its leaders are known to have made only moderate statements in favor of Pyongyang. First Secretary Sergey Kalyakin stressed to a visiting KWP delegation in August 1995 the importance of two of Kim Chong-il's works; and the following October, Secretary Viktor Chikin noted that the KWP was playing "*a* [not *the*] leading role in the international communist movement."[14]

The Delecration signing Communist Party of the Ukraine (KPU) appears similarly ambivalent. Its international secretary, was noted as lauding Kim Chong-il's *Socialism Is Science* while it was being distributed to every delegate to the party's Second Congress.[15] Just the same, a KPU delegation attended the 1996 PCF congress. The party is reported to be closer to the CP-RF than any other communist party of the former Soviet Union outside Russia.[16]

The fourth CPSU successor to have signed the Pyongyang Declaration, the Kazakh Socialist Party (KSP), in that it chooses not to use the term "communist" in its title. There is, moreover, a smaller Kazakh Communist Party on its Left, in a pattern typical of East European communist party successors (see below). The KSP is not important, however. But Chairman Bizanov of the ruling Kazakh People's Unity Party (PUP) was heard praising Kim Chong-il while receiving a KWP delegation in August 1995.[17]

Two possible Declaration signatories exist in Central Asia (our list is not complete). One is the, until recently, ruling Tajikistan Communist Party.

The latter is not known to have participated in the PCF system, and its chairman, Shodi Shabdolov, has stated during his April 1995 visit to that city that "Pyongyang is the only communist city of culture in the world."[18] Another possibly is the ruling Democratic Party of Turkmenistan. In spite of its name change, it has been described by at least one authoritative source as the most unchanged of any such party.[19] It did lend enough importance to its relations with the KWP to send its first secretary as leader of a party delegation to Pyongyang in July 1995. (Its more evidently pro-DPRK Ukrainian counterpart, incidentally, did so in February 1996.)

In South Asia

A second region of pro-DPRK/KWP strength, as in part determined by Pyongyang Declaration signers, is South Asia. In the first place, the two major Indian communist parties—the Communist Party of India (CPI) and Communist Party of India-Marxist (CPI/M)—were signatories. Though not the major Opposition parties in India, they were, as of 1990, two of the Free World's largest communist parties, being surpassed only by those of Italy and Japan.[20] Both parties participated in the PCF conference system as well. The CPI apparently leans more toward the PCF, for it enjoyed higher-level representation at the latter's last two Congresses, participates more frequently at its yearly *L'Humanite* festivals, and has (or has had) a representative stationed in Paris.[21]

The CPI-M, on the other hand, leans toward the KWP. To substantiate the latter observation, the North Koreans appear to have been the strongest foreign supporters of the CPI-M's May 1993 Marxism seminar in Calcutta, sending the largest delegation and providing the only head of state to greet it officially. CPI-M Secretary General H. S. Surjeet noted in April 1995 that "the changes on the international stage during the last three years clearly showed the validity of the idea and purpose of the Pyongyang Declaration."[22] Furthermore, a portrait of Kim Il-song was noted as hanging at the headquarters of the CPI-M's Center for Indian Trade Unions the following month.[23]

All this is logical in that the CPI-M has traditionally been the more radical of India's two major communist parties. It is also the more important since it rules the large state of West Bengal (73,000,000 people, which makes it larger than most countries of the world), the moderate-sized one of Kerala (30,000,000), and the smaller one of Tripura (3,000,000).

To illustrate the favorable environment in which all this took place, one should note that representatives of two very important Centrist Indian groupings, the normally-ruling Congress Party and the subsequently ruling Janata Dal, sent their secretary general and president, respectively, to the PCF Congress of January 1994. Also, the Congress Party had long been a mainstay of the communist front World Peace Council while the Janata Dal participated in the New Delhi "chuche" seminar of September 1990. This illustrates how more moderate elements belonging to the non-aligned movement are included in the World Revolutionary Process.

The Communist Party of Nepal, which is listed in *First Hand Information,* has been succeeded, for the most part, by the Communist Party of Nepal-United Marxist-Leninist (CPI-UML). The latter was one of the more outstanding signers of the Pyongyang Declaration. The CPI-UML was a ruling party during December 1994-September 1995 and remains a significant force in Nepal. During his tenure as prime minister, CPN-UML Chairman Man Mohan Adhikari said that his party and government "are finding the road to be followed by them in the famous works of dear leader Kim Chong-il."[24] Even the Nepalese king told a visiting KWP delegation that he hoped "to learn from the precious experience of Kim Chong-il."[25] Not to be left out, the leader of the Number 2 Nepalese communist grouping, the Workers and Peasants Party—small, but nevertheless represented in the legislature—stated during a July 1993 visit to the DPRK that the Pyongyang Declaration was the "banner of the international communist movement."[26]

Of the remaining *First Hand Information*, main-line communist parties in South Asia, all relatively insignificant, only that of Sri Lanka is known to have signed the Pyongyang Declaration. It, like the CPI-UML, was first noted as participating in the PCF conference system at the latter's 1996 congress.

What may be significant, and certainly surprising, is that the ostensibly moderate (and then governing) Pakistan People's Party (PPP), a consultative member of the *Socialist* International, also signed the Declaration, without participating in the PCF conference system. Even though relations between the KWP and PPP and their respective governments appear close in other ways, e.g., periodic exchange of delegations, etc., we have seen no immoderate pro-North Korean statements on the part of the Pakistanis. As in the case of India, a principal Oppositionist party to the Right of the country's main Pyongyang Declaration signer(s), in this case, the Muslim League, also maintains "fraternal relations" with the KWP.

The apparently insignificant People's League of Garib Newaz, which not only signed the Pyongyang Declaration, but also elected Kim Chong-il its honorary chairman in October 1995, is not to be confused with the currently-ruling Awami (People's) League of Sheikh Nasina Wajed (which was, however, represented at the 1990 PCF Congress and earlier on the aforenoted World Peace Council).

The Declaration-signing Workers Party of Bangladesh (WPBD), although also seemingly of little significance in its own country, is active internationally and a major vehicle for DPRK influence. For example, as of mid-1994, its secretary general, Rashid Khan Menon, doubled as chairman of the Bangladesh Committee for Supporting Korean Unification.[27] In spite of Bangladesh's proximity to both India and Nepal, the WPBD was the only party from its country to have attended the January 1993 CPN-UML Congress, the CPI-M's May 1993 Marxist seminar, or that party's April 1995 Congress.

Since we have information of an early 1993 joint statement of the *Communist* parties of Bangladesh, India, and Pakistan,[28] what we have in South Asia are two rival groups, a soft-line one oriented around the CPI and a hard-line one around the CPI-M and including the WPBD and possibly the CPN-UML, and CP Sri Lanka. While CPI-M, as we have previously noted, has a seemingly friendly orientation toward the KWP—a view reinforced by the position of the WPBD regarding both parties, we should be cautious in our approach. There is evidence of CPI-M's having equally close ties with *non*-Declaration-signing China and Cuba (see below). (Note that CPI-M leader Surjeet visited China for a week in late September 1997 at the Communist Party's invitation.)

In South West Africa

If we have two formerly ruling parties among the Declaration-signers in South Asia, we might say we have two and one-half presently ruling ones in South West Africa. The Popular Movement for the Liberation of Angola (MPLA), a "vanguard" party according to *First Hand Information*, the South West Africa People's Organization (SWAPO), a Soviet-style national liberation movement which came to power in Namibia in 1990, and the South African Communist Party (SACP), a *de facto* junior partner in its country's government since 1994, were the only African parties outside the relatively insignificant Peoples' Unity Party of Tunisia, to be original signers of the Pyongyang Declaration. This means they also had representatives in Pyongyang for the April 1992 Kim Il-song birthday celebrations.

Of the three, the SACP has probably been closest to the PCF (and thus most distant from the Koreans?). Not only was it the most frequent participant in the latter's conference system, but the visit of its president to Paris in April 1992 was the reason for the PCF's hosting a 10-party West European communist parties' meeting at the time. The PCF and SACP also co-sponsored a conference for "democratic African groups" in April 1995 and African participants in the *L'Humanite* festival the following September. SWAPO, on the other hand, may be the closest to the North Koreans. Its participation in the PCF conference system was the least of the three. Also, Namibia was the only country involved here noted as having presented Kim Chong-il with its highest decoration in February 1995.

The MPLA occupies a middle position with respect to the Korean and French communists. The real question is, how does this all relate to the party's alleged renunciation of Marxism-Leninism during the period between the December 1990 and May 1992 Congresses?[29] The MPLA, moreover, has continued its strong relations with the Cuban, Portuguese, and other communist parties.

"Greater Syria" Region

Another region of North Korean influence, as revealed by signatures to the Pyongyang Declaration, is Syria and the just offshore Cyprus. The latter has the most important Free World communist party signatory, outside of South Africa, Nepal, and India. Its Declaration-signing Progressive Party of the Working People (AKEL) is the major Opposition party on the island. The Syrian Ba'ath, a radical Marxist ruling party ("revolutionary democratic" by Soviet standards) signed the Declaration along with the bulk of the small Leftist parties in Lebanon, where Syria has massive influence, and in Jordan, where Syria is much less of a factor.

Neither the Syrian Ba'ath nor its much weaker Declaration-signing namesakes in Lebanon or Jordan (or Yemen, for that matter) participated in the PCF conference system, though the rival communist ("vanguard" party, in the case of Yemen) parties did. So, what we may have again in this situation are two Leftist groupings, one more oriented toward the North Koreans and the other toward the French Communists. This is comparable to the situation in South Asia. And the *Communist Party* of

Syria has (or has had) a representative in Paris, just as does its Indian namesake (see above).

Note that the Jordanian and Lebanese Communist parties, along with most of their Leftist compatriots, did sign the Declaration. However, Ba'athist-ruled Syria, it should be added, hosted the last (December 1994) Congress of the World Federation of Trade Unions (WFTU). At that congress, North Korea acquired a vice presidency and the Brazilian's a presidency. The new president, Antonio Neto, proved to be overly pro-Pyongyang while leading an unusually powerful delegation to that city in August the following year (not surprisingly, since his small General Confederation of Labor is controlled by the pro-North Korean MR-8—see above).[30] He stated that the exploits of the Great Leader Kim Il-song would be "immortal" and that "history does not know such a great man as the respected president who clearly disposed of his lifetime work (sic)."[31] (Meanwhile, the French communists have not occupied their vice presidential and secretariat posts on the WFTU, presumably to enhance their admission into the Centrist and influential European Trade Union Confederation.)

To what extent the Syrian government and its ruling Ba'ath Party were facilitating the increase of Korean influence in the labor organization is not known. However, it is clear that their favoritism toward Pyongyang is revealed by Syria's hosting one of three known overseas headquarters of the National Democratic Front of South Korea, a *First Hand Information* "vanguard" party, in Damascus. (The other two have been in Havana and Tokyo.) Also, on August 1995, Syria hosted an international conference of political parties and fronts in the Middle East and Arab Region supporting North Korea's 10-Point Program of the Great Unity of the Whole Nation.

Latin America

Latin America is the one large region where over half the *First Hand Information* parties signed the Pyongyang Declaration. It may have been the groundswell of pro-North Korean feeling in the region that led the Guadeloupe and Martinique Communist Parties, *de facto* subdivisions of the PCF, to sign. Nevertheless, in view of assumed PCF opposition to the North Koreans, it did seem strange.

The most important more or less contiguous area of Declaration support in this region is in El Salvador and Nicaragua. Here, the major Opposition parties, respectively, are the Farabundo Marti National Liberation Front

(FMLN) and the Sandinist National Liberation Front (FSLN); both signed the DPRK document. However, these two, as well as most of the Latin American *First Hand Information* parties, of which the FSLN, but not the FMLN, is one, also participate extensively in the PCF conference system.

The most surprising Declaration support in the Latin American region were certain parties of the English-speaking Caribbean plus Bermuda. These were declared socialists, not communist, and were non-participants in the PCF communist conference system. The now-ruling St. Kitts Labor Party (St.Kitts-Nevis), for example, was an original Declaration signer even though it is a consultative member of the Socialist International (just like the Pakistan People's Party—see above).

Two other original signers of the Declaration were the Progressive Labor Party (Bermuda) and the Dominica Labor Party, both of which are principal Opposition parties in their respective countries. The latter has been considered important enough to be in the Working Group of the influential Sao Paulo Forum (see below).

In Guyana, there was no participation from the traditionally communist, and now ruling, People's Progressive Party. However, the country's vice president (from the then-ruling People's National Congress) attended the April 1992 Pyongyang festivities for Kim Il-song's 80th birthday. In addition, the country's presumably small Amerindian Action Movement made Kim Chong-il its honorary leader in late 1995 (as did the Maurice Bishop Patriotic Movement of Grenada in early 1996). The North Korean affinity of these generally socialist parties of the English Caribbean, and of lesser Declaration-signing counterparts in the Bahamas, Barbados, Guyana, and Trinidad and Tobago as well, remains a puzzle.

A similar puzzle exists in the case of the Peruvian Left, most of which signed the Pyongyang Declaration. Only one of the eight signers, the Peruvian Communist Party (PCP), also participated in the PCF conference system. Though not as powerful as its counterparts in the Latin American countries mentioned above, Leftists in Peru, including the PCP and other Declaration signers, put together a coalition called the United Left (IU) and were, for a time, represented on the Sao Paulo Forum Working Group.

For his part, Peruvian President Fujimori received a KWP delegation soon after his assumption of office in 1990. Furthermore, in 1995, his Centrist Cambio 90 Party congratulated the KWP on its 50th anniversary. All this might be chalked up to diplomatic efforts to improve relations between the two countries, but the Peruvian honors given North Korean leaders have seemed somewhat excessive. Kim Il-song was made an honorary citizen of Cuzco in 1990 and of Ica and Huanavelica Cities (posthumously) in 1995. Kim Chong-il was made an honorary citizen of Pisco and Ica Cities in 1995 and of Nuevo Chimbote in 1996. He was also given honorary degrees by Chiclayo University in 1995 and San Pedro University in 1996. He was made an honorary professor of Huache National University (along with his late father) in the latter year. Equally bizarre were Left Revolutionary Union President Angel Castro Lavarello's characterization in August 1995 of Kim Chong-il as "the greatest of the great men"[32] and the pro-North Korean *The New Worker*'s favorable characterization of the Sendoro Luminoso on February 18, 1994. We thus see in Peru North Korean affinities that range from the Centrist government through the legal Left to the outlawed guerrillas.

The Surprising Non-Signers

At least three groups stand out as surprising for *not* having signed the Pyongyang Declaration: the traditionally communist ruling parties of China, Cuba, Laos, Vietnam, and, to some extent, Cambodia; the major non-Eurocommunist Free World Communist parties of France, Portugal, Greece, and Italy (the Refoundation Party); and the African parties that sent representatives to KWP-sponsored party-building seminars, ruled nations conferring their highest decorations on Kim Il-song or Kim Song-il, and/or had leaders making inordinate statements praising North Korea and/or its leaders.

Of all the non-signers noted here, the behavior of the Chinese Communist Party (CCP) is perhaps the easiest to understand. Given the relative size and traditional attitude of that country, any Chinese ruling party would be unlikely to want to appear to be taking direction from the North Koreans. In view of a growing and fruitful economic relationship between China and South Korea, why would the former want to antagonize needlessly the latter? But most importantly from our standpoint, the Chinese Communists appear to have undergone an ideological change with a resulting shift in strategic emphasis.

In the wake of the highly successful Chinese experiments with capitalism in contrast to the stinging criticism of capitalism by the April 1992 Pyongyang Declaration, the *Beijing Review* of January 4, 1993, felt it necessary to reiterate Deng Xiaoping's early 1992 call for the cessation of the "abstract debate" over what is capitalist and what is "socialist.[33] This was consistent with the previous (November 18, 1992) observation by Beijing's *Wen Wei Po* that the "East-West" (socialist versus capitalist) struggle had been replaced by the "North-South" (developed nation versus Third World) one as the main conflict in the world.

As if to drive home their differences, the North Koreans implicitly, and such Pyongyang mouthpieces as the minuscule Belgian Labor Party explicitly, have taken a jaundiced view of the new Chinese economic policy.[34] A scanning of the Foreign Broadcast Information Service's *Daily Report* for the period January 1992 through September 1993 found that, of the 70 some parties identified as having relations with the CCP, only about one-half were communist, but two-thirds were Third World; the two-categories, of course, are not mutually exclusive. If the Chinese do in fact have aspirations of leading the Third World, this is just another point of friction with the North Koreans, whose main objective is obviously to do the same. In spite of all this, North Korean media habitually give the Chinese pride of place, list its party and government first, and give it the most space when cataloguing attendance at Pyongyang meetings, receipt of congratulatory messages, etc. It is obvious that Pyongyang wishes to project as positive an image as possible of its relations with China.

If the non-signature of the Declaration by the CCP is the easiest to explain, the failure of the Cuban Communist Party (PCC) to sign is the most difficult. In 1990, at least one expert referred to Cuba as North Korea's "best Third World friend."[35] Just prior to the April, 1992, promulgation of the Pyongyang Declaration, Castro made a similar anti-imperialist and anti-capitalist pronouncement.[36] Cuba observed three days of official mourning following Kim Il-song's death in 1994 and gave Kim Chong-il its highest decoration in early 1995. Cuba's hosting of one of the few NDFSK offices abroad has been noted above. All these actions should have predicted that Cuba would be a signatory. It was not. The snub of not signing seems to have been repeated in late 1995, when Castro by-passed North Korea during his visit to China and Vietnam. North Korean sensitivity was probably manifest by Pyongyang's ostentatious celebration in early 1996 of the 10th anniversary of Castro's visit to that city.[37]

Cuban behavior could possibly be explained by its receipt of current aid from the PCF and its General Confederation of Labor (CGT) and potential aid from an increasingly prosperous China. These may have inhibited the Cubans from signing the Declaration or Castro from visiting Pyongyang. Besides, Cuba probably would not want to do anything to diminish the effectiveness of its extremely extensive and active international support mechanism, participated in by the broadest Left spectrum throughout the world and even by Centrist elements in Latin America. (See Chapter V below.)

The ruling Vietnam Communist and Lao People's Revolutionary parties, like the CCP and PCC, attended the 1982 Pyongyang celebrations without signing the Declaration. So did the three Cambodian political forces of the time: the royalist FUNCINPEC (senior governmental partner 1993-1997), the ex-(?)communist Cambodian People's Party (PPC) (junior partner 1993-1997), and the Oppositionist Khmer Rouge. The FUNCINPEC might have been expected to sign in light of King Sihanouk's excessive praise of Kim Chong-il (see above). Sihanouk was undoubtedly grateful for past North Korean hospitality in times of political adversity. FUNCINPEC also had extremely close relations with the KWP. For example, the FUNCINPEC was one of only two possible non-signers among the 14 parties attending Kim Chong-il's 51st birthday celebration in Pyongyang in 1993.[38] The PPC was supposed to have given up Marxism-Leninism in 1991, but it attended the PCF Congresses of 1994 and 1996 and was openly characterized as communist by a prominent CPI-M leader *after* it had taken over in July 1997.[39]

The Vietnamese party was unique in the Indochinese grouping in not sending its top leader to the 1982 birthday celebrations, while Laos, like Cuba, gave its top decoration to Kim Chong-il in 1995. Perhaps the residual PCF influence in Indochinese communism and/or the influence of a powerful neighboring China was/were responsible for the absence of Declaration signatories there. Even the ruling Mongolian People's Revolutionary Party (MPRP), though initially signing the Pyongyang Declaration in April 1992, rescinded its signature later in that year when it officially gave up Marxism-Leninism, a renunciation made more convincing by its failure, unlike the PPC, to attend the 1994 PCF Congress. (The MPRP did, however, send greetings to the October 1996 convention of the hard-line Communist Party U.S.A.)[40]

The relatively hard-line Communist Parties of Greece and Portugal, the Centrist ones of France and Italy (Refoundation), and Eurocommunist groups of Spain (United Left) and Greece (Coalition of Left and Progress) constitute the Communist Party Group in the European Parliament. The caucus-like Group was formed after the 1994 elections to that body. The Party Group works together, with the French party in the lead. For example, in May 1996, the PCF sponsored a high-level symposium in Paris on the effects of neo-liberalism and European unity on European Leftist employment. Not a single one of the 15 European Leftist parties represented had signed the Pyongyang Declaration, at least six were represented by their top leaders, including the heads of four of the parties just mentioned.

The PCF is far Left enough to have equivocated on the anti-Gorbachev coup attempt in 1991,[41] but far Right enough to have given up publicly on the principles of the "dictatorship of the proletariat" (authoritarian, one-party rule by the communists)[42] and "democratic centralism" (submission to the will of the "majority," but generally of the top party leadership)[43] as befits a party desiring credibility while operating in a parliamentary-democratic framework. This apparently enabled it to exercise some leadership over the relatively hard- and soft-line elements noted above. Significantly, the hard-line Portuguese and Greek parties are unusual in not having compatriot minuscule Pyongyang Declaration-signing parties on their Left; presumably there is no "necessity."

It is, of course, the relatively large size of the French Communist Party (PCF), its long experience in international affairs, and the wealth of its homeland that ultimately makes its leadership possible. Although the French party implicitly showed its disapproval of North Korea by being the most conspicuous absentee at the 1982 Pyongyang birthday celebrations (in contrast to modest KWP participation in PCF events), it was up to a small pro-Pyongyang European political party to state the true nature of the situation. In early 1994, the New Communist Party of Great Britain stated, in the context of the PCF's having dropped "democratic centralism" and failing to mention "socialism" in its new program, that "it is clear to many that it [the PCF} is not a communist party now."[44]

The unexplained rapprochement between the PCF and CCP at some time during 1992, among other things, tended to solidify the Opposition to the KWP. Earlier, the PCF had been sharply critical of the Chinese over the 1989 Tiananmen Square incident. This attitude lasted at least through the time of the January 1992 Congress of the communist-front International Union of Students (IUS).[45] But by the July 1992 visit to Beijing by *L'Humanite* editor Roland Leroy, the rift appeared to have been healed. The Chinese sent an unusually elaborate delegation to that newspaper's annual festival the following September.[46] By January 1994, there was so little PCF concern for the Chinese human rights record that the CCP could get away with sending the head of its Tibet unit as leader of its delegation to the party congress in Paris.

In Africa, things were a little different. Unexpectedly positive feelings for the North Koreans were not followed through with signatures to the Pyongyang Declaration, not even by the more radical political parties. In late 1990, a Second Seminar on Party Building was held in Tanzania for the Korean Workers' Party (KWP) and 13 ruling Black African parties plus the soon-to-be ruling African National Congress (ANC) of South

Africa. The presence of the KWP, the endorsement by the seminar of Kim Chong-il's *The Workers' Party of Korea Organizes and Guides All the Victories of Our People*, and the fact that the Seminar sent letters of appreciation only to Kim Il-song and the Tanzanian president pretty well mark it as a North Korean operation.

Of the 14 parties present, the Mozambique Liberation Front (FRELIMO) had been considered by the Soviets as a "vanguard" party, the Seychelles People's Progressive Front (SPPF) and Revolutionary Movement of Tanzania (CCM) as regular "revolutionary democratic" parties, and the ANC as a liberation movement.[47] All of these groups, plus four more—the Burundi Party of National Unity and Progress (UPRONA), the National Resistance Movement (NRM, Uganda), the United National Independence Party (UNIP, Zambia), and Zimbabwe African National Union-Patriotic Front (ZANU-PF)—have participated in Soviet-line international front organizations.[48] And all these except the NRM and UPRONA have participated in the PCF conference system, as has UPRONA's 1993 successor, the Democratic Front of Burundi [FRODEBU]. These eight parties may have considered signing the Declaration, but it may have been French governmental as well as PCF pressure that kept them from doing so. Of the remaining six, the People's Front of Burkina Faso (FPBF) also participates in the PCF system, but the ruling parties in Botswana, the Cameroons, Central African Republic, Madagascar, Uganda, and Rwanda do not.

A third party building seminar was held in early 1992 in Zimbabwe, hosted by the ruling ZANU-PF. It is assumed but not certain, in light of the previous seminar, that the other countries attending—repeaters Burkina Faso, Madagascar, Mozambique, Tanzania, North Korea, and Uganda, plus newly-attending Sierra Leone, Senegal, Egypt, and Tunisia—were all represented by their ruling parties. Of the new groups, not only does the ruling Socialist Party of Senegal participate in the PCF system, but the country has been unusually hospitable to international front organizations. Dakar is the site of the African regional center of the World Peace Council (WPC) and, in November, 1992, the place for holding the 16th General Assembly of the World Federation of Scientific Workers (WFSW, another communist front). The ruling All-People's Congress of Sierra Leone, like the Senegalese Socialist Party, also has had a history of front activity.[49]

Certain other African nations, not involved in these party-building seminars, gave their highest decorations to the Korean leaders: Zaire and Libya to Kim Il-song in 1992 and Equatorial Guinea, Mali, Namibia, and

Zaire to Kim Chong-il in 1995. African countries sending their chiefs of state to Kim Il-song's 1992 80th birthday celebration included decoration-giver Equatorial Guinea and seminar participants Sierra Leone and Guinea; 1990 seminar host Tanzania sent its vice president. But again, none of the ruling parties involved, except Namibia's SWAPO, is known to have signed the Pyongyang Declaration.

There are, however, some 47 Pyongyang Declaration signers we cannot identify. Probably the best chance we have for identifying some of these among the ruling African parties occurs in the cases of contiguous Ghana and Togo. We infer this in light of the August 1995 statements of some of their leaders. Secretary General Hudu Yahaya of the Ghanaian National Democratic Congress noted that "the Great Leader Kim Chong-il is a genius of ideology and theory."[50] Deputy Secretary General Dogbe of the Togolese People's Rally said that "Kim Il-song is the greatest man who devoted all his life to the victory of the independence of the oppressed people all over the world (sic)."[51] (This emphasis on Kim Il-song at that late date, however, may perhaps mask some reservations about Kim Chong-il.)

Uganda's de facto ruling NRM is yet another Declaration-signing possibility; its leaders rule the country, though political parties, per se, have been banned since 1986. In spite of the technical ban on parties, the *Pyongyang Times* of April 15, 1995, was able to report that the NRM's Political School had celebrated Kim Il-song's birthday and that of February 10, 1996, noted NRM National Political Commissioner Chango Machyo as a director of the International Institute of the Chuche Idea (IICI—see below). It goes without saying that the latter would not be in such a position without the approval of his party superiors. In this context, it should be re-emphasized that the NRM was virtually the only party-building seminar participant with a background in Soviet-line front activities that had not participated in the PCF conference activities noted in this study (see above).

North Korea and Front Activity

As for the traditionally Soviet-manipulated international fronts, mention has already been made of the DPRK's stepping into a WFTU vice presidency in late-1994 at the same time the French communists appear to have been cutting back on their participation in that organization. Another seeming increase in North Korean influence in this type of organization took place earlier, in 1992, when Pyongyang was made the site of the

Asia-Pacific Regional Center of the International Organization of Journalists (IOJ).

At home, much doubling up in front activities seems to have taken place on the part of North Koreans. Li Song-ho, described as vice chairman of the Korean Afro-Asian Solidarity Committee (KAASC), the country's affiliate of the Afro-Asian Peoples' Solidarity Organization (AAPSO) in 1988 and of the (identical or successor) Korean Committee for Solidarity with the World's Peoples (KCSWP) in mid-1995, was concurrently, as of the latter time, vice chairman of the Committee for Cultural Relations with Foreign Countries (CCRFC), apparently North Korea's focus for individual country and regional friendship associations and their counterparts abroad. The chairman of the KCSWP at this latter time was the recently-defected Hwang Chong-yop, the KWP secretary charged with foreign relations. Finally, also as of mid-1995, CCRFC Chairman Chong Chun-ki was concurrently chairman of the Korean Peace Committee, Korea's affiliate of the World Peace Council (WPC).

Such double-slotting was probably necessary in view of the fact that the DPRK runs a series of international fronts specifically concerned with itself in addition to participating in the full panoply of the formerly Soviet-dominated ones. Most unique here, but not surprising in view of the country's aforenoted concern with ideology and desire to spread it abroad, is the chuche study complex. As of early 1995, the North Koreans claimed over 1,000 such organizations in over 100 countries.[52]

The key coordinator here appears to be Tokyo's International Institute of the Chuche Idea (IICI), for one of its deputy directors general, Jose Francisco Aguilar Bulgarelli, is also director of the Latin American *Institute* of the Juche Idea while the other, Edmond Jouve, is president of the Council of the European *Society* of the Juche Idea. (The director general and secretary general of the IICI are both Japanese; there are also an Asian Regional Institute of the Juche Idea and an African Regional *Committee* for the Study of the Juche Idea; other units operate at the country, city, and institutional level.) The organization is highly professorial: Director General Inoue Shuhachi teaches at Rikkyu University; the aforenoted Deputy Director Jouve is at University of Paris (No. 5); three of the six identified IICI Board of Directors members teach at Lagos University (Alaba Ogunsanwo), the Central University of Ecuador (Milton Burbano), and Central University of Venezuela (R. J. Munes Tenotio), respectively; and the situation is repeated on down the line. Clearly, the DPRK has enlisted powerful intellectual support in this effort, but it is assumed that ultimate direction comes from the Academy of Chuche Science or Chuche Idea Academy (headed by one Li Ji-su and assumed to be in Pyongyang).

Two other DPRK international fronts are devoted to what appear to be the country's chief diplomatic objectives: re-unification on its own terms, and freedom to operate for its sympathizers in South Korea. At least these were the two main points of the Korean resolution passed at the aforenoted WFTU Congress of late 1994.[53] The International Liaison Committee for the Reunification and Peace of Korea (CILRECO, formerly the International Liaison Committee for the Independent and Peaceful Reunification of Korea) and the International Committee of Lawyers for Democracy and Human Rights in South Korea are both headquartered in France (Chatillon and Nice, respectively); both have French secretaries general (Guy Dupre and Robert Charvin, respectively); and they are interrelated; Charvin is also a CILRECO vice president. CILRECO at least is, like the IICI, organized on a regional and national basis. And just as the IICI has enlisted apparently high-level intellectual talent, CILRECO has, at least nominally, done so politically. Among its honorary chairmen are the formerly Number 1 leaders of Portugal (Francisco da Costa Gomes), Senegal (Leopold Senghor), and Malta (Dominique Mintos); the former mayor of Geneva and a Swiss Party of Labor (read: communist) Politburo member (Roger Dafflon); and the secretary general of the communist-front International Association of Democratic Lawyers (the Algerian Amar Bentoumi).

It is ironic that these Korean-oriented fronts are situated in Japan and France, whose communist parties have little or nothing to do with the KWP (see above). In Japan, it is the Socialist Party which seems to have the close connections with the North Koreans—frequent delegation contact, including the large, 134-member group attending the Kim Il-song 80th birthday celebration.[54] (This small party is not to be confused with the powerful Japanese Social Democratic Party, which was called the Socialist Party before its 1991 name change.) As for France, note that when a European regional DPRK friendship association was set up in January 1995, the Association for Promotion of European-DPRK Relations, it was done so in Paris with the former chief of staff of the French Armed Forces (Jeannou Lacaze) as chairman! And we have already noted that a Frenchman serves as one of only two known deputy directors general of the IICI. Still, we have no known Pyongyang Declaration signers in either Japan or France.

The situation is vastly different in IICI Deputy Director General Bulgarelli's Costa Rica. There, both the country's communist parties appear to have signed the Pyongyang Declaration without having participated in the PCF conferences noted herein. One of these, the Costa Rican People's Party (PPCR), elected Kim Chong-il its honorary leader in early 1996 and is the only party cited in *First Hand Information* that is known to have done such a thing. Bulgarelli heads the virtually unknown Popular Force Organized in Costa Rica, whose relationship to the PPCR cannot at present be determined. He appeared in the 1983-1986 *List of Members* of the communist front World Peace Council, as did CILRECO's Costa Gomez.[55] The latter, incidentally, was supposed to have described Kim Il-song as the most outstanding statesman and military strategist in the world[56] (coming from an ex-president and field marshal, this statement just might have credibility in certain quarters).

Notes

1. Pyongyang, KCNA, April 3, 1995 (FBIS, April 3, 1995), and September 7, 1995 (FBIS, September 7, 1995).

2. Ibid., September 19, 1995 (FBIS, September 22, 1995).

3. Ibid., September 6, 1995 (FBIS, September 6, 1995).

4. Ibid., October 12, 1995 (FBIS, October 13, 1995).

5. Ibid., November 22, 1995 (FBIS, November 28, 1995).

6. See the author's "The Communist Movement and Its Allies," in Ralph M. Goldman (ed.), *Transnational Parties* (Lanham, MD: University Press of America, 1983), pp. 28-39.

7. Pyongyang, KCNA, February 19, 1995 (FBIS, February 22, 1995).

8. Ibid., September 16, 1995 (FBIS, September 19, 1995).

9. Radio Pyongyang, August 17, 1995 (FBIS, August 21, 1995).

10. Ibid., January 28, 1995 (FBIS, February 1, 1995).

11. *Sovetaya Rossiya*, (Moscow), April 26, 1997.

12. Moscow, Radio Rossii Network, April 220, 1997.

13. *Pyongyang Times*, November 26, 1994.

14. Pyongyang, KCNA, August 21, 1995 (FBIS, August 22, 1995), and October 24, 1995 (FBIS, October 26, 1995).

15. *Pyongyang Times*, June 3, 1995.

16. S. S. Simonsen, "Leading the Communists Through the 90's,"

Transition (Prague), July 14, 1995, p. 63.

17. Pyongyang, KCNA, August 25, 1995 (FBIS, August 28, 1995).

18. Ibid., April 21, 1995 (FBIS, April 21, 1995).

19. RFE/RL, *Research Report*, January 22, 1993.

20. Richard F. Staar (ed.), *1991 Yearbook on International Communist Affairs* (Stanford: Hoover Institution, 1991), pp. xxiii, xxxiv.

21. *L'Humanite* (Paris), September 14, 1991 and September 17, 1996.

22. Pyongyang, KCNA, April 3, 1995 (FBIS, April 4, 1995).

23. *Pyongyang Times*, May 20, 1995.

24. Pyongyang, KCNA, March 5, 1995 (FBIS, March 8, 1995).

25. Ibid., March 2, 1995 (FBIS, March 8, 1995).

26. Ibid., July 29, 1993 (FBIS, July 30, 1993).

27. *The People's Korea* (Tokyo), June 11, 1994.

28. *New Age* (New Delhi), March 14, 1993.

29. Arthur S. Banks, Alan J. Day, and Thomas C. Miller (eds.), *Political Handbook of the World* (Binghampton, NY: CSA Publications, 1996), p. 30.

30. U. S. Department of State, telegram from Asuncion dated December 1, 1994, quoting *Jornal do Brasil* (Rio de Janeiro), November 29, 1994.

31. Pyongyang, NCNA, August 9, 1995 (FBIS, August 10, 1995).

32. Ibid., August 11, 1995 (FBIS, August 11, 1995).

33. Geng Yuxin, "A Changing China and Changing World, *Beijing Review*, January 4-10, 1993, p. 4.

34. Beijing, AFP, November 2, 1992 (FBIS, November 3, 1992); *People's Democracy* (New Delhi), June 20, 1993.

35. Wonmo Dong, "Democratic People's Republic of Korea," in Richard F. Staar (ed.), op. cit., p. 191.

36. *Granma* (Havana), April 12, 1992.

37. Pyongyang, KCNA, March 8, 1996 (FBIS, March 12, 1996).

38. *The People's Korea* (Tokyo), February 27, 1993.

39. *People's Democracy* (New Delhi), September 21, 1997.

40. "World Communists Greet CPUSA," *Political Affairs* (New York),

March 1996, p.34.

41. "European Communists Off Balance," *Facts on File* (New York), August 29, 1991, p. 643.

42. "Communist Parties Discuss Collapse of Soviet Union," *Links* (Broadway, NSW, Australia), April-June 1994, p. 121.

43. *The New Worker* (London), April 8, 1994.

44. Ibid.

45. *People's Democracy* (New Delhi), February 9, 1992.

46 "Parties communistes d'Amerique latine renis par le PCF," *Horizons Nouveau* (Paris), October 1992, pp. 29-30.

47. Author's "The Communist Movement and Its Allies," op. cit., pp. 33-36.

48. See World Peace Council, *List of Members, 1983-1986* (Helsinki: WPC Information Centre, undated), and *VIIth AAPSO Congress* (New Delhi: Congress Reception Committee, 1988), pp. 196, 202; *The 13th Session of the AAPSO Council* (Cairo: Afro-Asian Publications, 1981), p. 374; *The XIVth Session of the AAPSO Presidium* (Cairo: Afro-Asian Publications, 1988), p. 112.

49. *VII AAPSO Congress*, op. cit., p. 202; World Peace Council, op. cit., pp. 140-141.

50. Radio Pyongyang, August 17, 1995 (FBIS, August 21, 1995).

51. Pyongyang, KCNA, August 12, 1995 (FBIS, August 15, 1995).

52. Ibid., April 10, 1995 (FBIS April 11, 1995).

53. U. S. Department of State, telegram from Seoul dated December 5, 1994, quoting Pyongyang, KCNA, December 5, 1994.

54. Radio Pyongyang, April 16, 1992 (FBIS, April 16, 1992).

55. World Peace Council, op. cit., pp. 61, 137.

56. Pyongyang, KCNA, August 14, 1995 (FBIS, August 15, 1995).

Chapter 3

The French Communists as
Premier Conference Hosts

The mere attendance at a conference sponsored by the French Communist Party (PCF) does not involve the degree of commitment that signature to such a document as the Pyongyang Declaration does. This might go a long way toward explaining why, of the some 106 communist parties noted in *First Hand Information*, about 83 (or their successors) are recorded as having participated in the PCF conference system while only 38 (after multiple successor organizations in the former Soviet Union and former Czechoslovakia are discounted) originally signed the Declaration. If participating "vanguard" parties are compared, the result is much more one-sided: seven "vanguards" in the PCF system and only one (Angola) favoring the Declaration.

Though the respective totals for PCF conference participants and Declaration signers are roughly 250 and 235 (see Appendix II), most of the latter, as noted earlier, are relatively inconsequential. Another positive interpretation of the higher PCF numbers is the realization that the financial resources required for attendance at a conference from beyond the Europe-North Africa-Middle East region represents some degree of commitment, whether paid for by the foreign party or subsidized by the French.

The triennial congresses of the PCF have supplanted those of the old CPSU as the largest of their kind. The 27th PCF Congress of December 1990 was attended by 110 foreign delegations.[1] The 28th Congress of January 1994 had approximately 140 delegations,[2] and the 29th about 160,[3] indicating, of course, that these meetings represented more of a front gathering rather than one of just communists. Virtually all elements of the World Revolutionary Process were present. Comparative figures for other recent and important party conferences are as follows:[4]

Cong-ress	Host Party	Date	Foreign Delegations
[27th	Communist Party of the Soviet Union	Feb 86	152]
1st	Sandinist National Liberation Front ("vanguard")	Jul 91	93
4th	Cuban Communist Party	Oct 91	none
14th	Chinese Communist Party	Oct 92	none
14th	Portuguese Communist Party	Dec 92	50
3rd	Communist Party, Russian Federation	Jan 95	47
15th	Communist Party of India-Marxist	Apr 95	20
8th	South African Communist Party	Apr 95	39
14th	Spanish Communist Party	Dec 95	52
15th	Communist Party of Greece	May 96	67
3rd	Reforundation Communist Party of Italy	Dec 96	c.100
4th	Communist Party, Russian Federation	Apr 97	82
15th	Chinese Communist Party	Sep 97	none

The annual festivals of the PCF's newspaper, *L'Humanite*, are large for their kind of event. The festival of September 1995 had some 96 foreign delegations, whereas that of the Portuguese Communist Party's *Avante* that same month had only about 40 despite the fact that many attendees could have made the short trip from nearby France.

Efforts to exert PCF leadership may have been manifest in the pattern of regional conferences held alongside the *L'Humanite* festivals. The 1990 congress was used as a springboard for an Arab communist parties meeting and the 1991 one for such European and Mediterranean groups. The festival of 1992 evoked one for the Latin American delegations present. The festival of 1995 was paralleled by a meeting for the African attendees. The 1992 Latin American meeting was of special interest since it focused on the Chinese view of "North-South" struggle (see above). The meeting occurred just after the Korean Workers Party (KWP) delegation had attended, and possibly directed, a Latin American communist party meeting in Quito (March), the Pyongyang Declaration was promulgated (April), and another KWP delegation succeeded in picking up 20 signatures for that document at the Sao Paulo Forum meeting in Managua (June). (See Chapter V, below).

The 1995 African meeting was of interest because of the key role played in it by South African Communist Party Deputy Secretary General Jeremy Cronin.[5] The meeting was reminiscent of the 1992 West European communist parties meeting that the PCF staged in honor of SACP President Joe Slovo.

Further evidence of PCF involvement in these regions were newspaper accounts of the 1994 congress and 1994 and 1995 festivals. These reports indicated that, of the 35 parties represented at these events that had permanent representatives stationed in France, four were from the Arab World, nine from Latin America, and 19 from Black Africa. Of the latter, all but three were Francophone.[6] This latter figure lends weight to the idea that PCF influence may have been responsible, to some extent, for the failure of otherwise friendly Black Africans to sign the Pyongyang Declaration.

Turning to regional conferences for areas of which France is a part— Western Europe and the Mediterranean, we again see evidence of French initiative. The PCF-sponsored May, 1996 "Progressives of Europe" meeting on unemployment produced a kind of "who's who" of West European communism. The top nine communist parties plus far Left parties more important than their minuscule communist compatriots, particularly in Denmark and Norway, and at least seven secretaries general or their equivalent attended. The 10-party West European communist parties meeting of April, 1992, sponsored by the PCF to welcome South African Communist leader Joe Slovo, had one (German), possibly two (also British?) Pyongyang Declaration signers, which was a slight difference from the May, 1996, meeting.

In February, 1991, the PCF co-sponsored in Tunis, with the Pyongyang Declaration-signing Tunisian Communist Party, a Mediterranean "progressives" meeting. The following September, it sponsored the aforenoted meeting of European and Mediterranean Left (mainly communist) parties attending the *L'Humanite* Festival that had the potential of five Declaration signers among a total of some 20 parties attending.

What we may have in these circumstances, tentatively speaking, is the PCF gradually withdrawing contact with parties that signed, or would eventually sign, the North Korean document in this region: from co-sponsorship with one party (February, 1991), a possible 25 percent (September 1991), 10 or 20 per cent (April, 1992), none at all (May, 1996).

One sympathetic commentator noted in June, 1995, the existence of an "international Scandinavian Left-socialist current" consisting of the very four parties from that region that attended the PCF-sponsored meeting in May 1996: the Left Party of Sweden, the Socialist People's Party of Denmark, the Socialist Left Party of Norway, and the Left Alliance of Finland.[7] In 1993, a mutually exclusive communist group from this region (*all of which had signed the Pyongyang Declaration*) had issued a joint statement calling for the withdrawal of foreign troops from Yugoslavia; they were the Workers Party Communists of Sweden, the Communist Forum of Denmark, the Norwegian Communist Party, and the Communist Workers' Party of Finland.[8] Thus, we add to the evidence information regarding PCF versus DPRK-oriented groups previously noted in the cases of "soft" versus "hard" communists in South Asia and communists versus Ba'athists in the Middle East.

What is less clear is how much, if at all, two West European communist parties to the Left of the PCF were seeking to undermine the efforts of the latter even as they worked with the PCF and had not signed the Pyongyang Declaration. The Portuguese Communist Party (PCP), described by one commentator as "the most Stalinist of the West European communist parties,"[9] had hosted a significant meeting in May 1992 that consisted of the six most powerful communist parties in Western Europe (if one considers Cyprus in Western Europe): parties from Portugal, Spain, France, Greece, Italy (Refoundation), and Cyprus. The latter, the only Pyongyang Declaration signer here, was also the only foreign party that sent its secretary general. There was no repeat meeting.

Similarly, the Portuguese hosted the February, 1995, Assembly of the World Federation of Democratic Youth (WFDY), traditionally the fourth largest of the international communist front organizations. However, the PCP did not seem to move in on it the same way as the PCF did in the meeting of the Women's International Democratic Federation (WIDF). The latter, traditionally the third largest of the fronts, elected a PCF

National Committeewoman as its president while holding its April, 1994, Congress *in France*. In addition, it moved its headquarters from East Berlin to Paris! Two other communist fronts, the World Federation of Teachers Unions and the Trade Union International Chemical Workers, moved their headquarters from Eastern Europe to France during the 1991-1992 period. Finally, by 1997 the at least formerly influential World Peace Council(WPC) appeared to have moved its headquarters from Helsinki to that of its French affiliate in Paris.

Thus, the Portuguese communists are not giving their French counterparts much competition. Just the same, their *relatively* pro-North Korean stance, as befits a more radical party, must provide at least a minor irritant to the latter. For example, apparently unlike the PCF, the PCP did bother to send a delegation to the 1992 Pyongyang Kim Il-song birthday celebration. Further, in conjunction with hosting the 1995 WFDY Assembly, the Communist Youth of Portugal co-sponsored with the international a "World Youth Conference to Support the Reunification of Korea."

The case of the Communist Party of Greece (KKE) is more complicated. Described by 1991 as definitely hard-line by one commentator,[10] it applauded the August, 1991, coup attempt against Gorbachev whereas the PCF equivocated.[11] It had been previously concerned with the Eastern end of the Mediterranean and points farther east; e.g., its May, 1992, 4th Regional Meeting of the Communist Parties of the Middle East and Mediterranean did not include any countries west of Greece, and its December 1994, conference at least had a title that referred to "Communists and Leftists of the Mediterranean and Black Sea Regions." It may, however, have come into competition with the PCF in June 1995 when it also incorporated West European groups in a conference it hosted for 26-36 parties (accounts vary).

In retrospect, the *Le Monde* (Paris) coverage pictured this meeting as a hard-line rival to the one held in Paris in May, 1996.[12] At the time, that newspaper noted the uncompromising "no third way between socialism and capitalism" aspect of the 1995 meeting. The attendance of the British, German, and Finnish Communist Parties, the Refoundation Communist Party of Italy (RPCI), the AKEL of Cyprus, the Communist Party-Russian Federation (CP-RF), and the Tudeh of Iran, and the absence of the French, Chinese, Cuban, and Portuguese communists, was apparently cited as evidence supporting this contention.[13] The latter four parties did indeed participate in the PCF conference system without having signed the

Pyongyang Declaration, but the same is true of the Tudeh and RPCI. The CP-RF, AKEL, and the German Communist Party (DKP) signed the Declaration, but also participated in the PCF conference system. So did the Communist Party of Britain, if it were the party to which the term "British Communists" referred to. This leaves only the Finns; we do not know whether the Communist Party-Unity (PCF conference system only) or Communist Workers Party (Pyongyang Declaration only) is indicated here. Since we do not have the complete list of delegates, we must say that "the jury is out" on this one, especially in view of the absence of the Portuguese Communist Party, *like the KKE, an important non-Declaration signer to the Left of the PCF,* which has failed to renounce the "dictatorship of the proletariat."[14]

The picture is much more clear cut in Eastern Europe than in either Western Europe or the former Soviet Union (see above and Chapter 2). In general, the "reformed" communist parties, where they are active internationally, have minimal relations with the PCF and did not sign the Declaration, but smaller parties usually retaining the communist label have just the opposite set of relationships. The exception is Hungary, where the ruling Socialist Party (a full Socialist International [SI] member) relates to the PCF and not to the Declaration all right, but where the Left splinter and Declaration-signing Labor Party appears to have even closer relations with its French counterpart (based on frequency and level of contact). Thus, the whole political situation is shifted Rightward here, just as it is shifted Leftward in Russia, where even a party to the Right of the main line CPRF has signed the Declaration (see above).

The until recently ruling Bulgarian Socialist Party and Social Democracy of the Republic of Poland participate in the PCF system and are flanked on their Left by the small, Declaration-signing Bulgarian Communist Party-Bulgarian Communist Party-Marxist complex and Polish League of Communists (Proletariat), respectively. The government-supporting and PCF-participating Romanian Socialist Labor Party is similarly flanked on its Left by the small, Declaration-signing New Socialist Party-Party for the New Society complex. Then, the PCF-participating Albanian Socialist Party (ruling from 1997), Communist Party of Bohemia and Morovia, and Slovak Party of the Democratic Left have small, Declaration-signing compatriots in the Albanian Communist Party, Czech Party of Communists, and Slovak Communist Party. (Whereas the ruling Serbian Socialist Party attended the PCP's *Avante* Festival of September 1995, the RPCI Congress of December 1996, and the CP-RF one of April 1997, we have no record of its attending any of the 1990 to 1997 PCF conferences noted herein.) In any case, all this indicates that the PCF certainly is ascendent over the North Koreans in Eastern Europe as in Western, though its degree of involvement, based on frequency and level of contact, appears definitely less in the former than in the latter. (See Appendix II.)

The formerly East European Party of Democratic Socialism (PDS), the new name for the old, ruling Socialist Unity Party (SED) of East Germany, fits this pattern of a relationship with the PCF; it is as close as any party to it, based on frequency and level of contact (see Appendix II). There is even a PCF-PDS Commission for Development and Exchange of Cooperation. It also failed to sign the Pyongyang Declaration.

The fact that the large and important Japan Communist Party also failed to sign the Declaration comes as no surprise in view of its traditional "Eurocommunist" positions. PCF strength is impressive in the Arab World, where it has conference participants in the following countries, with no apparent Pyongyang Declaration signers: Algeria, Bahrain, Egypt, Iraq, Oman, Palestine, and the Sudan. (The same, incidentally, is true for Haiti, Iran, Israel, New Caledonia, and the Philippines.)

This imbalance is most spectacular in Black Africa, where the North Koreans appear to have considerable support short of Declaration adherence. This will be gone into in more detail presently. Meanwhile, we should note that PCF Third World strength, as evidenced by participation in its party conference system, crops up in the very same three regions earlier noted for specialized conferences in conjunction with *L'Humanite* festivals and party representatives in Paris: the Arab world, Latin America, and Black Africa.

The following Black African countries had PCF conference participants, but virtually no known Pyongyang Declaration signers: Burundi (ruling party), Cameroon, Cape Verde (chief Opposition party), Central African Republic, Chad (a relatively unimportant "vanguard" party), the Comoros, Djibouti, Equatorial Guinea (chief Opposition party), Ethiopia (formerly ruling party, now defunct), Gabon, Ivory Coast, Mozambique ("vanguard" ruling party), Niger (junior partner in ruling coalition), Reunion (PCF extension), Rwanda (ruling party), the Seychelles (ruling party), Somalia, Tanzania (ruling party), Togo (ruling party), Western Sahara (liberation movement), and Zimbabwe (ruling party).

The PCF conference system also had Black African ruling party participation in the following countries which had other parties signing the Pyongyang Declaration: Mali, Zambia, and Senegal. The Senegal case is especially interesting, for its ruling Socialist Party (SSP) and its two *First Hand Information*-listed communist parties all participated in the PCF conference system without having signed the Pyongyang Declaration while a fourth party there signed the Declaration only. The SSP, although a *full* member of the Socialist International, has, through its government, been a stalwart supporter of international communist front organizations. For example, as noted in Chapter 2, Dakar is the site for the African regional center of the World Peace Council (WPC), traditionally the largest and most important of the international communist front organizations. The city also hosted the November, 1992, Congress of one of the lesser fronts, the World Federation of Scientific Workers (WFSW), which President Abdou Diouf incidentally lauded at the time for "having resisted any form of ideological pressure."[15] (And in mid 1996 Diouf was noted in rejoicing that "the great President Kim Il-song's course is being brought to completion under the wise guidance of His Excellency the great Kim Chong-il".)[16]

This leads one to wonder how much full membership in the SI will guarantee moderate behavior on the part of the others in this category of participants in the PCF conference system: the Moroccan Socialist Union of Popular Forces, the (now-ruling and formerly communist) Italian Democratic Party of the Left (PDS), and the Progressive Socialist Party (PSP) of Lebanon. The latter is, of course, most suspect in this connection. A long-time participant in international front activity and ally of the Communist Party of Lebanon, the PSP had, incredibly for a full SI member, also signed the Pyongyang Declaration. But then, so had another party in that category, the February Revolutionary Party of Paraguay.

Notes

---

1. *L'Humanite* (Paris), 19 December 1990.

2. Ibid., January 26, 1994.

3. Ibid., December 20 adn 21, 1996

4. Richard F. Staar (ed.), *1987 Yearbook on International Communist Affairs* (Stanford: Hoover Institution, 1987), p. xxix; *Barricada* (Managua), July 22, 1991; *Avante* (Lisbon), December 10, 1992; *People's Democracy* (New Delhi), February 5, 1995, April 23. 1995,

January 14, 1996, and December 29, 1996; *Green Left Weekly* (Broadway, NSW, Australia), April 26, 1995; and *The New Worker* (London), June 21, 1996.

5. *L'Humanite*, September 19, 1995.

6. Ibid., January 26 and September 10, 1994 and September 16, 1995.

7. *Green Left Weekly* (Broadway, NSW, Australia). June 28, 1995.

8. *People's Weekly World* (New York), October 9, 1993.

9. Arthur S. Banks, Alan J. Day, and Thomas C. Muller (eds.), *Political Handbook of the World: 1995-1996* (Binghampton, NY: CSA Publications, 1996), p. 771.

10. Ibid., p. 365.

11. "European Communists Off Balance," *Facts on File* (New York: August 29, 1991), p. 643.

12. *Le Monde* (Paris), May 12-13, 1996.

13. Ibid., June 20, 1995.

14. "Communist Parties Discuss Collapse of Soviet Union," *Links* (Broadway, NSW, Australia), April-June 1994, p. 121.

15. *Le Soleil* (Dakar), November 11, 1992).

16. *The People's Korea* (Tokyo), June 1, 1996

Chapter 4

Links as the International Marxist Periodical

Links magazine, issued more or less quarterly, first appeared with an April-June, 1994, issue. It seems to be the closest thing to a successor of the *World Marxist Review* (*WMR, Problems of Peace and Socialism*) monthly, which ceased publication with a double, May-June, 1990, issue. Like the *WMR* in the past, *Links* purports to be a forum for Marxist discussion promoting the unity of the participants. Unlike the narrowly Moscow-line *WMR*, the new magazine avowedly seeks pluralism, inviting participation from "pro-Moscow communist parties, Trotskyist parties, Maoism, the left wing of nationalist movements, left forces breaking with social democrats, and activists from social movements who have come to realize the need for a party" (e.g., environmentalists and feminists). It draws the line at "Stalinism" on the one hand and social democracy *per se* on the other.[1]

The magazine's Editorial Board reflects this attempted diversity, with the following representation: the host Australian Democratic Socialist Party (DSP), an ex(?)-Trotskyist group; the Sri Lankan Nava Sama Samaja Pakshaya (NSSP, the New Social Equality Party), currently Trotskyist; the Indonesian People's Democratic Party (PDR), a probable "left wing of a nationalist movement"; the New Zealand Alliance and British Militant Labour as "left forces breaking with social democrats"; the Filipino

MAKABAYAN and BISIG and American Committees of Correspondence (CoC), Rightist *de facto* splinters from rather hard-line established communist parties—the Filipino one with a Maoist history and the American one as a traditional Pro-Moscow group; the German Party of Democratic Socialism, a "reformed" main-line communist party extremely close to the PCF; and the South African Communist Party (SACP), the one-pro-Moscow party coming over intact as a former *WMR* participant. The last named party is currently involved with disparate Left elements, e.g., a signer of the Pyongyang Declaration that is not only a participant in the conference system of the French Communist Party [PCF], but also a close collaborator of that party in its Black African affairs. (See Chapter 3).

The SACP is the only party with such widespread outside contacts. With these across-the-board connections, the two Left splinters from Right (Socialist) parties and the two Right splinters from Left communist ones seem to have a "dead Center" average within the extreme Left, particularly if we omit the Trotskyists. We infer that the Trotskyist goal is to promote Leftist unity around this kind of Centrist constellation. *Links* is being used as a vehicle for just this goal, with the willing collaboration of the SACP, a group strong enough to resist being manipulated by the other parties represented.

The idea of such a Centrist effort comes through with the magazine's statement that it favors a "democratic, non-authoritarian socialism while equally opposing capitalism and imperialism."[2] Of course, the former is intrinsically opposed to North Korea's authoritarian domestic conduct while the latter is an exact reflection of North Korea's foreign policy as expressed in the Pyongyang Declaration. Again, this is a kind of averaging out a Centrist position between the two ideological poles.

This Centrist position, as well as the mix that produced it, is seen in *Links'* enthusiastic coverage of the Danish Red-Green Alliance in its October-December, 1994, issue. This grouping is composed of the (Eurocommunist) Left Socialist Party (VS), the (Trotskyist) Socialist Workers Party (SAP), the (formerly Moscow-oriented) Danish Communist Party (DKP), and the (formerly-Maoist) Communist Workers Party (KAP)—a true "dream team" by *Links* standards. The *Links* article went on to state that the Socialist People's Party (SF), the party chosen by the PCF to represent Denmark at the May, 1996, meeting in Paris (see Chapter 3), had "moved to the Right." Of course, neither the Communist Forum, which was the leading Danish signatory of the Pyongyang Declaration, nor the other two Danish parties that signed that document were members of the Red-Green Alliance. This would seem as good an example as any of a breakdown between North Korea, the PCF, and *Links* within the world's Marxist movement.

The fact, however, that the Alliance-member DKP *and* the "Rightist" SF *and* the Leftist Communist Forum were all represented at the 1992 *L'Humanite* festival lends weight to the contention that attendance at PCF meetings *per se*, especially on the part of Europeans, is not conclusive evidence of ideological orientation.

On March 22, 1995, *Links'* sister publication, *Green Left Weekly*, took up this same theme. It approvingly cited the New European Left Forum's desire of "creating/expanding *the new space to the left of the Social Democrats and separate from what are described as the traditional/unreformed Communist parties.*" The New European Left Forum, it added, arose out of the initiative of the Spanish United Left (IU), which an earlier issue (February 22, 1995) had described as including the Trotskyist Alternative Left (since 1993) as well as the dominant Eurocommunist Communist Party of Spain (PCE).

The previous year (August 17, 1994) *Green Left Weekly* had approvingly reported the formation of a 15-party National Democratic Alliance in Mexico, centered on the Democratic Revolutionary Party (PRD), third strongest and major Leftist party in the country. The PRD had earlier absorbed the Eurocommunist Mexican Socialist Party and later joined with the Trotskyist and *Links*-participating Revolutionary Workers Party (PRT) in the National Alliance. The latter occupies a position between the mildly Leftist and ruling Institutional Revolutionary Party (PRI) (which had sent its secretary general to the PCF Congress of 1994 and joined the Socialist International [SI] in 1996) and the Pyongyang Declaration-signing Popular Socialist (PPS) Party. This is comparable to Spain, where the United Left is situated between the mildly Left and, until recently, ruling Spanish Socialist Workers' Party (PSOE) (SI affiliate) on the Right and the Pyongyang Declaration-signing Communist Party of the Peoples of Spain (PCPE) on the Left.

The history of the formation of the Committees of Correspondence (CoC) reveals that it contains within itself the type of alliance *Links* is promoting. CoC finds itself between the Pyongyang Declaration-signing Communist Party USA (CPUSA) on the Left and the SI-affiliated Democratic Socialists of America (DSA) and Social Democrats USA (SDUSA) on the Right. The core of CoC was the 1991 breakaway faction from the CPUSA. The faction was Rightist in that it called for more inner party democracy, pragmatic in that it wanted the party to be more flexible, and racial in that it involved most of the CPUSA's Black leadership (Angela Davis being the best known bolter).

This CPUSA splinter was then joined by activists from the DSA ("left forces breaking with social democrats"), Trotskyists from both the Socialist Workers Party and Solidarity, feminists from the National Organization of Women, Greens, and others. Ever since its First Annual Conference in July 1992, the CoC's external contacts were largely limited to other *Links* contributors; exceptions were attendance at the Congresses of the PCF. In fact, foreign delegates to the CoC's June, 1994, Second National Convention were limited to *Links* contributing editors from the German PDS and the Brazilian PT, the Australian DSP's editor of *Green Left Weekly*, the CPSA's secretary general, and a relatively unknown Cuban communist. With this background, it is not surprising that the CoC, with its four Editorial Board members and two contributing editors, makes the second most important input to *Links*, after the Australian DSP.

The non-authoritarian stance of the magazine is somewhat suspect when one considers its Cuban connection, however. The whole Cuban relationship here is curious, as it is, incidentally, with the North Koreans. (See Chapter 2.) Of course, if nothing else, it exemplifies the magazine's stated dedication to presenting contrasting viewpoints.

Though the Cuban consul attended the March-April, 1994, Green Left Conference in Sydney that launched the magazine, no one else from the island came to the meeting. Cuban contributing editors and articles did not make their appearance until Issue No. 4 (January-March, 1995). This issue had *two* articles by new contributing editor Juan Antonio Blanco. In one, he stated: "Referring to the organizational and conceptual elements of real socialism that the Cubans imported and 'tropicalized' and which still exist in the island's structure. . . , it would be ridiculous to expect that their destiny will be any different from that of their European paradigms."[3] He then goes on to hope for a "revolutionary" development into a different form of "socialism." All this was much in keeping with *Links'* stated position.

Blanco is described as director of a "Cuban non-governmental organization," so that the appearance of an opposing view by a Central Committee employee and member of the Cuban Communist Party (PCC) in the very next issue (No. 5, April-June, 1995) has some degree of surface logic. However, it is not credible that Blanco would hold his job without government and party approval. In this second article, Dario Machado justifies at great length and idealizes Cuba's one-party system.[4]

It should be noted that an unsympathetic source has stated that the *Links*-hosting DSP "maintains close links with the Castro regime in Cuba and is the center of a number of pro-Cuba organizations in Australia"[5] and that the "world class" Trotskyist economist Ernest Mandel was, until his 1995 death, at the same time *Links'* most renown contributing editor and a good friend of Fidel Castro.[6] Also, the main Trotskyist grouping—the Fourth International-United Secretariat (FI-US)—participated in the November, 1994, Cuban international solidarity meeting in Havana. Finally, we should add that the PCC, to the extent that it is represented in the roster of *Links* contributing editors, is its one other intact connection with the old *WMR,* the SACP being the other.

The Mandel connection and the DSP's Trotskyist background bring up the question as to just how much influence this Marxist tendency wields over the magazine and to what extent the latter is a vehicle for the former. The DSP, which not only hosted the formation of the magazine, but also provides its managing editors—it is assumed that Nichols is a member of DSP—and, presumably, its headquarters site, was the Socialist Workers Party (SWP) until late 1989, which may or may not be related to the blow-up in Eastern Europe. Neither the DSP nor the SWP was listed in the *Political Handbook of the World, 1995-1996,* which gives some idea of their domestic importance. The SWP, originally spawned by its American namesake, had broken with the FI-US in 1985. In view of the subsequent close ties between FI-US and *Links,* one wonders if the break was not merely a formal one meant to facilitate the party's work with a wider range of organizations. Besides, the DSP was a guest at the July, 1995, 14th Congress of the FI-US.

As for *Links'* contributing editors, Mandel headed the whole FI-US as well as its Belgian affiliate, presumably the Workers's Revolutionary League (LRT?). The other Belgian contributing editor, Francois Vercammen, is also a leader of both groups. Contributing editor Alain Krivine heads the FI-US affiliate in France, the Revolutionary Communist League(LCR), while his Mexican counterpart on the magazine, Hector de la Cueva, is a leader of the Fl-US-affiliated Revolutionary Worker's Party. Contributing editor Dulce Maria Pereira of the Brazilian Workers' Party (PT) may or may not have been a member of one of the Trotskyist groups that went into that organization. But, note again, the PT *per se* was a guest at the 1995 FI-US Congress. So was the Refoundation Communist Party of Italy (RPCI), whose Luciana Castellana is yet another *Links* contributing editor. Finally, contributing editor James Petras of the American CoC was active in a Trotskyist front organization in 1969.[7] If one gives full credit for the DSP's contributing editor Pat Brewer and Mandel (deceased), Vercammen, Krivine, and de la Cueva, and half credit to Pereira, Castellana, and Petras, we arrive at roughly a one-third Trotskyist input at this level.

At the higher level, that is, the Editorial Board, the Trotskyist influence is even more pronounced if one considers the three DSP members plus the two DSP managing editors in this category. It is assumed that Sri Lankan Editorial Board member Sunil Ratnapriya is a member of the Trotskyist NSSP, since the secretary general of this party was the one Sri Lankan observed at the Green Left Conference at which the magazine was launched. The secretary general also wrote the one article on that country that has appeared in *Links* (No. 4). CoC Editorial Board members Peter Camejo and Malik Miah are two of the Trotskyists who came into this party after the core group split with the CPUSA. Phil Hearse was identified as a FI-US member at the founding Green Left Conference[8], although as a Militant Labourite (ML) in his subsequent article for *Links* [No. 5). Militant Labour accepted a *Links* Editorial Board slot by early 1996,[9] and by the middle of the year, Lynn Walsh was occupying it. However, it is not certain to what extent ML is an *officially* Trotskyist split from the British Labour Party. This accounts for over one-half of the Editorial Board with Trotskyist backgrounds. It should be added that the Filipino BISIG, which is represented by Editorial Board member Francisco Nemenzo, was also a guest at the 1995 FI-US Congress.

As alluded to earlier, the SACP appears to be *Links'* major connection with the orthodox communist world. With the death of Mandel, Editorial Board member Jeremy Cronin may well be the most noteworthy person on the magazine's staff. He is the deputy secretary general of this successful, fast-growing party. He also edits its quarterly *African Communist*. The party is a junior partner in the South African government by virtue of its immersion in the much broader African National Congress (ANC), again, the sort of thing *Links* would applaud.

Cronin's aforenoted brokering of Black African contacts for the PCF suggests he may also be the latter's window into *Links* as well. However, the Party of Democratic Socialism (PDS), an allegedly reformed successor of the old, ruling Socialist Unity Party of East Germany, at the same time also furnishes an Editorial Board member to the magazine while appearing to be one of the closest associates of the PCF, that is, if frequency and level of contact is any guide. (See Appendix II). At the very least, we can say that the PCF has some good friends here.

The fact that the SACP represents a Black country no doubt pleased the strongly black CofC. SACP's Black secretary general Charles Nqakula was the ranking foreigner at CoC's June, 1994, convention (see above). Furthermore, perhaps the CoC's well-known co-chairperson and 1968 CPUSA presidential candidate, the Black Charlene Mitchell, reciprocated at the CPSA Congress of April 1995.

To what extent the SACP—or the Cubans, for that matter—influence two other main-line parties represented on the roster of *Links* contributing editors—the (Nicaraguan) Sandinista National Liberation Front (FSLN) and the (Salavadoran) Farabundo Marti National Liberation Front (FMLN)—is not known. The former was listed as a "vanguard" party by *First Hand information* in 1988 while the latter absorbed the orthodox Communist Party of El Salvador in 1995. Jorge Shafiq Handal headed the latter; he continues to be important in the former. They are the chief Opposition forces in their respective countries and, thus, probably stand ready to make some impact on *Links*.

More relevant with respect to any CPSA connection in this context, these two Central American organizations, like the African party, are in that rather small group of Pyongyang Declaration signers who also participate in the PCF conference system. This pattern is more common in Latin America than elsewhere. It seems as if success, as well as the aura afforded by being close to one's own revolution, gives one entree across the whole far Left spectrum.

It is in the field of personnel that we find perhaps the most startling difference between *Links* and the *WMR*. The Editorial Board until just recently consisted of all English-speaking persons, mostly as a primary language and possibly secondary language in the cases of Sri Lanka and the Philippines. The addition of a German and Indonesian by mid-1996 has changed this. This may in fact have been one of the criteria for membership on the Board, since none of the additional parties and institutions represented among the contributing editors, with the exception of the Malaysian, appear generally to produce such personnel. This was logical for a magazine published only in English, which is a difference from *WMR*. Of course, the coverage of *Links* is worldwide, although the first seven issues plus a scanning of the list of contributing editors suggests that China and Northeast Asia, the Middle East, and Africa outside of the

Republic of South Africa may have been slighted. The Filipino Editorial Board members, however, provide a linguistic link to the other Malay on the Board (Indonesian), the other Asian person on the contributing editors list (Malaysian), the Australian Max Lane and the American Malik Miah. The latter are mentioned because of their special interest in Indonesia. Lane edits *Suara Aksi* (Bulletin of Indonesian Solidarity) and Miah, *Indonesian Alert*, but whether this involves any Indonesian language capability is not known. Peter Camejo, a Latino member of CoC, possibly gives the Editorial Board a Spanish-language capability. Thus far, however, translations from that language have only involved co-managing editor Dick Nichols, presumably an Australian who also speaks French.

Aside from the, until recently, linguistic uniformity of its Editorial Board, *Links* personnel also differ from those on *WMR* in that none of the non-Australians, neither Editorial Board members nor contributing editors, appear to work at the magazine's headquarters. No doubt advances in computer technology make this a much more tenable situation than would have been the case in the days of the *WMR*. The consequences seem to be twofold. Some high-level foreigners can afford to take positions with the magazine and be actively engaged in it, and rather senior Australian officers of the magazine are sometimes saddled with its workaday tasks. In contrast, the resident staffers at *WMR* headquarters were, on the average lesser ranking, at the alternate Central Committee level.

The high-level positions of Editorial Board member Cronin (South Africa) and contributing editors Mandel (Belgium) and Krivine (France) have already been mentioned. To these two must be added the following Editorial Board members: Sonny Melencio (vice president of MAKA-BAYAN), Francisco Nemenzo (chairman of BISIG), and Carl Bloice (a co-chairman of CoC). Also to be added are the following contributing editors: Dulce Maria Pereira (a PT member of the Brazilian Senate) and Manning Marable (another CoC co-chairman). As for top Australian staffers doing workaday tasks, co-managing editor Dick Nichols has already been mentioned as working at Spanish and French translations.

While it cannot match the resources of the *WMR*, which had representatives of each participating party at its Prague headquarters. *Links* does have access to the foreign correspondents of *Green Left Weekly*, the DSP newspaper that preceded it. So far, *Links* seems to have made use only of *Green Left* correspondents Renfrey Clarke (Moscow) and Stephen Marks (Managua). However, it has the potential of calling on such persons stationed in the following important cities: Amsterdam, Auckland, Berlin,

Boston, Budapest, Jakarta, Johannesburg, London, Mexico City, Port Moresby, Prague, Suva, The Hague, and Wellington.

To sum up, *Links*, in spite of its claims to a broad-based Marxist pluralism, seems primarily focused on Trotskyist and formerly Moscow-line communists. The Cubans may be part of the glue that holds this together, with their traditional affinity for foreign Trotskyists and its propaganda support from them, at the same time functioning as Moscow-liners, albeit sometimes reluctantly. In any case, the magazine's participants and those supported by it almost invariably fall into the space between main-line Socialist Parties on the Right and medium to hard-line Communist Parties on the Left. It thus represents a middle way between the exclusively PCF conference participants on the one hand and exclusively Pyongyang Declaration signers on the other.

As an aside, there is evidence of prior collaboration among the parties involved in *Links* on a regional basis. This leaves aside prior worldwide cooperation among the Trotskyists involved. In 1990, on the initiative of PT, the Sao Paulo Forum was launched. This involved three of the four of *Links'* Latin American parties. The Cuban Communist Party, the FSLN, and the FMLN were three of the six major players in that grouping. *Links'* Mexican affiliate, the Revolutionary Workers Party, later became allied to a fifth major Sao Paulo Forum element, the PRD (see above). This Latin American alliance remains the most successful of the "New Left" organizational efforts in the post-Berlin Wall era. (See Chapter V.)

In another instance, in June, 1993, virtually all of *Links'* continental West European components were involved in an Assembly of the European Left, with Mandel, Krivine, and representatives of both the German PDS and Italian RPCI in attendance.[10] The latter is a left splinter from the old Italian Communist Party (PCI), the main body of which became the SI-affiliated Democratic Party of the Left (PDS) and helps rule the country.

There are probably other examples of pre-April, 1994, regional cooperation between what were to become *Links* participants. (Among Australian and New Zealand components? Among American and South African ones?). The function of *Links* was to facilitate their cooperation on a worldwide basis.

Notes

1. "Introduction," *Links* (Broadway, NSW, Australia), April-June 1994, p. 3.

2. Ibid.

3. Dr. Juan Antonio Blanco, "Cuba, the Jurassic Park of Socialism?," op. cit., January-March 1995, pp. 96-99.

4. Dario Machado, "Development, Democracy, and Socialism in Cuba," op. cit., April-June 1995, pp. 16-17, 20-25.

5. "Trotskyite DSP Conference," *Social Action* (Melbourne), February 1994, p. 10.

6. *The Times* (London), 25 July 25, 1995.

7. U.S. Senate, Committee on the Judiciary, *Trotskyite Terrorist International*, July 24, 1975, p. 67.

8. "International Workers' Movement News," *Links* (Broadway, NSW, Australia), July-September 1994, p. 124.

9. *Green Left Weekly* (Broadway, NSW, Australia), February 14, 1996.

10. "International Workers' Movement News," *Links* (Broadway, NSW, Australia), April-June 1994, p. 127.

Chapter 5

The Playout in Latin America

Just as the Left was collapsing in Eastern Europe and the Soviet Union, it appeared to have begun to take on new life in Latin America. As *Links* (August-October, 1995) and the Cuban Communist Party's (PCC) *Granma International* (June 14, 1995) could agree, Latin America's Leftist forces did better than ever during the elections of November 1993-May 1995. The subsequent issue of *Links* (January-April, 1996, November-December not being covered) cited as Leftist victories during this period the following: two presidencies (Haiti and Panama), three governmental coalition junior partnerships (Bolivia, Chile, and Venezuela), and "more than 300 deputies, 60 senators, various governors, hundreds of mayors, and thousands of counsellors." The Haitian "victory" was a 1994 re-imposition by U.S. troops of a 1990 election result.

Standing outside this time-frame were the victories [with premierships] of a reformed communist party in Guyana (October, 1992) and a Pyongyang Declaration-signing socialist one in St. Kitts-Nevis (July, 1995). Prior to these electoral successes and possibly related to them was the formation of what appears to have been the most successful organization of the Latin American Left ever, the Sao Paulo Forum, in July, 1990. The same year saw the reinstitution of a series of Latin American communist party meetings, possibly competitive with the Forum, but certainly complementary to it. Both these organizational initiatives appear to have been spurred on by a heightened fear of a United States no longer counter-balanced by the Soviet Union and its former allies, a fear no doubt compounded by the suspected U.S. role in the unexpected Sandinista defeat in Nicaragua in early 1990.

The Sao Paulo Forum

The very broadly Leftist Brazilian Workers' Party (PT) was the instigator and host of the first Sao Paulo Forum meeting in the city of that name. Though attended by 47 other parties of the Latin American Left, the event was controlled by the PT. Its final document criticized not only America's "neo-liberal [economic] offensive" (a criticism that could have been expected), but also *the lack of democracy in Cuba*.[1] This was in contrast to subsequent Forum pronouncements. The PT has had a history of *Links*-style anti-authoritarian pronouncements.[2] Even at the 1996 meeting of the Forum, *in the midst of adulation for Cuba*, PT International Secretary Marco Aurelio Garcia stated that Cuba "is not a model or paradigm for us."[3]

Aside from the leverage obtained by the PT from being the sponsor of the Forum and host of its first meeting, its influence was no doubt magnified by having previously won the Sao Paulo mayoralty (1988) and by its leader, Luis Ignacio ["Lula"] da Silva, having just come in second in the country's presidential race (1989); and after the Forum's inauguration, the PT went on roughly to double its number of Deputies (1990). And while the PT has continued to increase its electoral strength as Brazil's predominant Leftist force, it did not develop as fast as its more optimistic supporters had hoped and thus never seems to have recovered the prestige it had at the time of the Forum's founding. For example, "Lula" again came in second in the 1994 presidential elections in spite of help from other members of a Leftist coalition. The party placed only fifth in the number of national Chamber and state Assembly seats won in 1995.

While *Links*, in line with its PT editorial contributor, apparently had some doubts about democracy in Cuba (See Chapter 4), in its wrap-up report on the 1995 meeting of the Sao Paulo Forum (No. 6), it could state:

> . . . [I]t has been the example provided by Cuba of the reality of an alternative system, which had brought the movement together for five meetings. It is difficult to imagine the Forum playing the role it does today, if

indeed it would even exist, without the existence of the Cuban revolution.[4]

This was quite a tribute (and revelation), if true. It is at least partially substantiated by the Salvadoran press' reports of the overriding adulation of Cuba at the Forum's meeting of July 1996.[5] In fact, by the time of the Forum's second meeting (1991) in Mexico City, Cuba had become one of six members of its Working Group. In 1993, Havana itself hosted the meeting. The 1997 meeting was in Porto Alegre (with a PT mayor), ending the expectation that a new host might emerge.

The two positions—early Working Group membership and meeting host—reflected just who the main powers in the organization were, especially in light of delegation activity at the meetings themselves, Other than the PT and Cuban Communist Party (PCC), the parties meeting this criteria were: Democratic Revolutionary Party (PRD) of Mexico (1991), Sandinista National Liberation Front (FSLN) of Nicaragua (1992), Broad Front (FA) of Uruguay (1995), and Farabundo Marti National Liberation Front (FMLN) of El Salvador (1996). There was no 1994 meeting.

Bolstering the main-line communist influence of the Cubans in the Forum were the facts that the FSLN was characterized by the Soviets in their authoritative *First Hand Information* (1988) as a "vanguard" (near-communist) party, that the PRD and FMLN had since absorbed the main-line communist parties of their respective countries, and that the Communist Party of Uruguay (PCU) is the Number 2 power (after the Socialists) in the FA. Not only is the PT unique among these six groups in not having an orthodox communist connection, but it is the weakest of any in its own country. The PCC, of course, rules. The FSLN is ambiguously partially ruling and, at the same time, is the chief Opposition force. The FMLN is clearly Number 2 in El Salvador. The FA (or more specifically, the Progressive Encounter of which it is a part) is roughly tied for that position in Uruguay, and the PRD is Number 3 in Mexico.

The PT is likely to remain some sort of force in the Forum, however, for at least three reasons. First, there is the sheer size of Brazil, which makes even a fifth place position substantial in absolute terms. Second is its connection with the Trotskyist Fourth International-United Secretariat (FI-US) and the current vitality of the latter. We have already discussed such sources of current FI-US strength as its connection with *Links* magazine and the Cubans. Third, Sao Paulo was chosen in 1995 as the site for the Forum's permanent Secretariat.

In discussing the 1993 Forum, the Trotskyist (but non-FI-US affiliated) *Militant*, journal of the American Socialist Workers Party (SWP), criticized the PRD for being pro-capitalist and excessively concerned with "electoral contests in the hope of taking over the reins of capitalist government." It also criticized the FMLN and FSLN for having moved "Rightward" and lauded the "Cuban revolutionaries" for not having given up the "Socialist option." *Militant* carried the same line in discussing the 1995 Forum while adding the FA to the PRD category. The PT was not included among the "bad guys" in 1993 and received outright favorable treatment from *Militant* in its coverage of the 1995 meeting; that of 1996, however, finally placed them in the enemy camp[6], leaving only the Cubans among the major players as "pure."

The FI-US' *International Viewpoint* made a somewhat parallel criticism of the 1995 Forum, castigating that body's majority for being wedded to a parliamentary struggle over and against a virtuous minority committed to "social confrontation."[7] That *Viewpoint* was also favorable to the Brazilian party at that time is supported by the fact that the same issue of *Viewpoint* chose Forum delegates from the PCC, *PT*, and Uruguayan Tupamaros to present their views on the Mexican Zapatistas.[8] All this is rather ironic in that Castro, in spite of having continually enunciated the superiority of "socialism over capitalism," stated at the 1993 Forum that parliamentary politics rather than armed struggle was the future way for the Left to go in Latin America[9] and that the PT has had the relevant involvement in parliamentary politics.

The first regular article in the first issue of *Links* (April-June, 1994) is an interview with FSLN Secretary General Daniel Ortega. The first question asked of him concerned the Sao Paulo Forum. This demonstrated the importance the magazine attributed to the Forum and, possibly, the trust it put in Ortega's proper evaluation of it. Ortega came down squarely in favor of the Forum's position that the East-West (socialist versus capitalist) struggle has been replaced by the North-South (developed capitalist countries versus Third World) one as the major dynamic in the world today. He also endorsed a subordinate theme in Forum declarations: that controlled experiments with a market-style economy, as currently undertaken in China and, allegedly in Vietnam and Cuba as well, are O.K.[10] These interview comments are in direct contradiction to FSLN behavior observed during 1992 when, as host to the Forum in July, it not only signed the Pyongyang Declaration, but allowed a Korean Workers' Party (KWP) observer delegation to secure 19 more signatures from those present.[11] (Recall that the Declaration defends socialism against imperialism and capitalism.).

On October 16 that same year, the FSLN's *Barricada* maligned the Chinese by stating that it was difficult to tell the difference between their "market socialism" and its "capitalist twin." All this might relate to the *Militant*'s complaint as early as August 23, 1993, that the FSLN had shifted "Rightward." The *Militant* gave as other examples two groups it had attacked in this context, the PRD and FMLN, as being "soft" on the Clinton Administration. With respect to this particular, however, it spoke favorably of the FSLN working with the Cubans to effect a compromise statement regarding U.S. policy. The "heroes" in this debate, as portrayed by *The Militant*, were the Uruguayan communists, *partners of the Tupamaros* in the FA.

In any case, the entire Forum movement seems to have been an ideological victory for the Chinese. The Chinese have attended at least some of its meetings in the role of observer, but their *direct* influence has not been obvious. As noted earlier, the Chinese were taking the position that the North-South struggle was replacing the East-West one as the major political dynamic in the world and were showing impatience with socialist versus capitalist ideological discussions. China's successful experiments with a controlled market economy and its greater number of party contacts with Third Worlders than communists *per se* were putting this new orientation into practice.

The Forum's *de facto* focus was on the U.S. as the "main enemy" in this context: first, as blockader of Cuba; then, as monopoly-capitalist economic predator in all of Latin America; next, as intervener in Panama and occupier of Puerto Rico, and, finally, as a menace outside the Latin American area. On the latter point, Somalia, North Korea, Libya, Palestine, and Iraq were cited in the Forum's 1993 Declaration (see Appendix III). All this fit contemporary Chinese policy. A CCP joint Political Committee and Central Military Commission document of late 1993 reiterated that the U.S. was still the main enemy.[12]

In view of the French Communist Party (PCF) 1992 rapprochement with its Chinese counterpart and the PCF's increased involvement in Latin America, we might expect some involvement by PCF on behalf of what appears to be the Chinese-endorsed line. Not only did the PCF sent observers to the Forum, but its virtual appendage, the Communist Party of Guadeloupe (PDG), was admitted to the Forum's Working Group in 1994. Also, three of the Forum's *powers*—the PT, FSLN, and FMLN—were among the 13 Latin American parties that had offices in Paris during the

1990-1995 period.[13] The payoff was the conference on the North-South issue that the PCF staged for the Latin American delegations participating in its *L'Humanite* Festival during September 1992. This festival could be seen as directly competitive to the KWP's successful efforts in Managua to secure 20 more Latin American signatures to its East-West-struggle Pyongyang Declaration at the July 1992 meeting of the Forum.

Two more recent additions to the Forum's Working Group should be noted as potentially influential in view of their status as ruling parties: the Haitian Lavalas Political Organization (OPL) and the Panamanian Democratic Revolutionary Party (PRD). They were admitted in 1993 and 1994, respectively. Their impact on the Forum has not yet been noteworthy and, in fact, neither attended the 1995 meeting. Lavalas leader Jean-Bertrand Aristide has in the past been more stridently anti-American than Rene Theodore, his counterpart in the United Party of Haitian Communists (PUCH).[14] Both of these Haitian groups have been limited participants in the PCF conference system. We have little feel for the PRD, except to note the implications of the *Granma International* (Havana) August 9, 1995, notation that "relations with Panama [were] improving greatly" (the PRD had come to power the previous May) and the KWP's greetings to the PRD's December 1995 5th Congress.

Before leaving the subject of the Sao Paulo Forum we should mention the larger meetings that expanded its influence. These were a series of "Latin American and Caribbean Conferences for Solidarity, Self-Determination, and Life of Our Peoples" in Quito (1988), Bogota (1989), Sao Paulo (1991), and Havana (1994). Not limited to their political party delegates, which largely duplicated those of the Forum,[15] participants also represented "trade unions, peasant organizations, student federations, women's rights groups, and environmentalists."[16] The Havana meeting of January, 1994, was said to have had nearly 1,200 delegates. This was up from 250 in 1988 and well over the 400 attending the 1993 Sao Paulo Forum in the same city.[17] In other words, these conferences had all the attributes of a front operation, although for a wider Left spectrum than merely communist parties.

In sum, we can say that of the six main powers in the Sao Paulo Forum, all but the PT have strong ties with traditional communists. Five, all but the FA, participate in the PCF conference system. Three, possibly four—PCC(?), FLSN, FMLN, and PT—furnish contributing editors to *Links* magazine. Only three—FA, FMLN, and FSLN—also signed the Pyongyang Declaration. Furthermore, the latter's adherence to the North

Korean position was in doubt in view of its apparent post-1992 policy changes.

Trotskyist influence is probably felt through the PT subdivision of that orientation and the longstanding affinity of that strand of communism for the Cubans. The policy enunciated by the Forum is at the very least entirely consistent with that of the Chinese communists and may have resulted to some extent from the efforts of the CCP's PCF ally. The overriding anti-Americanism of the Forum's members finds itself manifested primarily through parliamentary and similar forms of non-violent struggle. Allowance is certainly made for guerrilla activity in certain cases, as evidenced by the admission of the Guatemalan National Revolutionary Unity (UNRG) to the Forum's Working Group in 1993 and the presence of the National Guerrilla Coordination Simon Bolivar (CNGSB) of Colombia among its "over 100 member organizations," the figure given in *Links* in early 1996.[18] It is not known if the 112 members cited by the *New York Times* (July 29, 1996) coverage of the Sixth Forum includes such Latin American observers as the Institutional Revolutionary Party [PRI] of Mexico.

Communist Party Meetings

The first two Latin American communist party meetings of 1990 preceded the foundation of the Sao Paulo Forum and seemed to presage it. This undoubtedly fit with the orthodox communist connections of five of the six political parties that have since dominated the Forum. While reaffirming support for "scientific socialism" and attacking "imperialism," the February meeting in Quito of 10 South American parties called for the unity of the Leftist and Centrist forces of the region.[19] This meeting was impressive in that virtually all the main-line South American communist parties attended except that of Guyana, whose Marxist credentials were beginning to become suspect anyway.[20] The meeting was considered important enough to attract observers from the Cuban Communist Party, the FMLN, the FSLN, and, presumably, the PCF, PCE, and KWP. *Granma International* listed "France, Spain, and *South* Korea, the latter believed to be an editorial slip.[21] It was surprising, then, that the USSR, China, and Vietnam did not attend. However, these three, along with the North Koreans, were observers at the Latin American communist parties' meeting of November 1990 and the First Sandinista (FSLN) Congress of July, 1991)[22]

The secretaries general of five Latin American and Caribbean communist parties—Costa Rica, the Dominican Republic, Honduras, El Salvador, and Argentina—signed an open letter calling for a *broad alliance* (italics mine) for "democracy and self-determination" that entailed a "firm defense" of Cuba and "solidarity" with the FMLN and FSLN. Argentina represented the only overlap with the Quito meeting the month before.

The open letter was carried in the 26 March *Barricada* (Managua) of March 26, with no mention of where the meeting, if any, had taken place. Havana's *Granma International*, on March 30, carried a dispatch dated the 29th reporting individual statements by three of the very same leaders: Shafiq Handal of El Salvador, Rigoberto Padilla Rush of Honduras, and Narciso Isa Conde of the Dominican Republic, along with Secretary General Eduardo Caceres Valdivia of the Unified Mariateguista Party of Peru, supporting Cuba's protest of the "telegresion" of Radio Marti's TV broadcasts. According to the *Yearbook of International Communist Affairs: 1991*, there was a *meeting* of Latin American communist parties in Havana in March which spoke of an "acute crisis of the bureaucratized socialist models that became highly authoritarian and repressive."[23] If such a meeting and statement were true, it would have been reason enough for the Cubans not to have publicized it!

In any case, the subsequent Latin American communist party meetings were antithetical to the Forum. This was not surprising. The North Koreans were involved in all three. Two (November, 1990, and March, 1994) were officially sponsored by the Pyongyang Declaration-signing Popular Socialist Party (PPS), the rival of the Sao Paulo Forum's PRD for the affections of the Mexican Left.

To complicate matters, the PPS is also an admirer of the Forum's Cuba, to which it gave $50,000 in 1992.[24] This contrasted with the coolness in PRD-PCC relations observed in 1990.[25] The fact that Cuba sent a low-level delegation to the 1990 meeting, even though Cuban solidarity was one of its main themes, and apparently did not participate at all in the 1994 gathering, bring to mind Cuba's snub of North Korea by refraining from signing the Pyongyang Declaration in 1992 and having Castro fail to visit that city during his 1995 trip to the Far East.

By having more than half of the *First Hand Information* Latin American parties plus observers from the ruling parties of the USSR, China, Vietnam, and North Korea attending the 1990 meeting,[26] its PPS host was obviously endorsed by these powers as *the* communist party of Mexico. The Mexican Socialist Party, as identified in *First Hand Information,* had been absorbed into the PRD in 1989. The PPS was also the sole Mexican representative at the Calcutta Marxism seminar in May, 1993, sponsored by the Communist Party of India-Marxist (CPI-M) and endorsed by KWP. At the Calcutta meeting, the PPS delegate called for the "establishment of socialism and communism in Mexico."[27] This was a position well ahead of the Sao Paulo Forum's and in accord with the Pyongyang Declaration. In April, 1995, PPS Central Committeeman Roberto Prado declared that the birthday of Kim Il-song "is the most significant day of the people of the world advocating socialism can never forget (sic)."[28]

Without having any direct factual information, we can only infer that the Quito meeting of communist parties in March, 1992, had all the earmarks of a KWP enterprise. The timing was such that it occurred the month preceding the promulgation of the Pyongyang Declaration. We do know that efforts were made by the KWP to secure Latin American signatures to the document at the July, 1992, Forum meeting, three months after its proclamation. As it happened, from the only party list we have for the occasion, [29] all six parties who thought the Quito meeting important enough to sent their secretaries general later adhered to the Pyongyang Declaration. Only one of them, the Peruvian Communist Party, also participated in the PCF conference system.

The theme of the meeting was party building, a favorite subject of Kim Chong-il and the topic of known KWP-sponsored meetings in Africa (see Chapter 2). Like the Pyongyang Declaration, it rejected any accommodation with capitalism and any idea that "socialism" had ceased being a viable system.[30] This meeting, incidentally, was the same size as the 1990 one in Mexico City. Both were said to have had 17 Latin American delegations, but there was a repeat attendance apparently in only 10 of the cases by the communist parties of Argentina, Brazil, Chile, El Salvador, the Dominican Republic, and Peru; the PPS of Mexico, the Popular Vanguard Party of Costa Rica, the Panamanian People's Party, and the National Guerrilla Coordination Simon Bolivar of Colombia (which included the Communist Party).[31]

While we do not have detailed information on the 1994 conference, sponsored by the PPS in Mexico City, there were several differences from the 1990 conference. The Communist Party of Canada (CPC) and Communist Party USA, but not its more moderate rival, the *Links*-connected Committees of Correspondence, made it a hemispheric rather than a strictly Latin American meeting. Observer delegations from outside the hemisphere included only the ever-present Korean Worker's Party, the insignificant Tudeh Party of Iran, and the important CPI-M. The inclusion of the two Anglo-American parties had no doubt been prepared by the PPS-sponsored meeting of the three parties in Mexico City just a year before, in March, 1993. Similarly, the groundwork for the CPI-M participation was probably laid at the PPS attendance at the Indian party's May, 1993, Marxist seminar in Calcutta.

The CPI-M participation is interesting, but not surprising, in view of its affinity for the North Koreans. This Indian party, furthermore, shares with the PPS a strong attraction to the Cubans. CPI-M Secretary General H.S. Surjeet has been touted as "Cuba's best friend in India."[32] It was probably the Havana location of the Sao Paulo Forum in 1993 as much as anything else that brought him there. He was not known to have attended any of the other meetings; if he did, he certainly did not play a leading role. The CPI-M was clearly the spark plug for the September, 1995, Asia-Pacific Regional Encounter of Solidarity with Cuba held in the CPI-M stronghold of Calcutta. The Encounter was inaugurated by West Bengal's CPI-M chief minister, Jyoti Basu. Earlier, it had been the CPI-M's Center of Indian Trade Unions that sponsored the Cuban support resolution at the 1994 Congress of the communist-front World Federation of Trade Unions (WFTU).[33]

What is surprising is the lack of a major role played by the English-speaking Caribbean groups with a pro-North Korean orientation. The Pyongyang Declaration-signing Labor Party of Dominica, however, was placed on the *Sao Paulo Forum*'s Working Group in 1994. Grenada's Maurice Bishop Patriotic Movement, which elected Kim Chong-il as its honorary chairman in 1996, is a *Forum* member in good standing. The explanation is, perhaps, that none of these groups is, strictly speaking, a communist party. The two parties possibly in the communist classification—the ruling (since 1992) People's Progressive Party (PPP) of Guyana and the minuscule Workers' Party of Jamaica—significantly moderated their policies by 1990 and neither has been active internationally since that year. Nevertheless, in September 1997, CPI-M leader E.M.S. Namboodiripad openly cited the PPS as a "party of the working class," i.e., communist.[34]

Strictly Cuban-Support Activities

In contrast to the presumed *rivalry* between the pro-KWP PPS and the more strictly communist party complex just described on the one hand and the pro-PCF, pro-Chinese Communist Party (CCP) elements dominating the Sao Paulo Forum on the other was the *cooperation* of all these elements in activities supporting Cuba. This followed from the fact that both groups generally supported the Cubans, even though the Cubans themselves tended not to support each side equally. Nowhere was this better demonstrated than at the November, 1994, Havana "First World Solidarity Conference with Cuba, "which featured former PCF Secretary General Georges Marchais and *de facto* (if not *de jure*) KWP Foreign Secretary Hwang Jang-yop among its estimated 3,000 or more delegates.[35] Other notable parties at this meeting were those governing China, Vietnam, South Africa, Angola, and Mozambique. Also in attendance were the Sao Paulo Forum powers from Brazil, El Salvador, Nicaragua, and Mexico. Additional *Links*-supporting groups were from Germany, Italy, and the FI-US. The latter's magazine gleefully observed that the Socialist International and the Greens were absent.[36]

This conference was followed by the Asia-Pacific Cuban-support meeting in Calcutta. A similar one occurred in Johannesburg for southern Africa. Both took place in late 1995 and both were self-described as the "first" of their kind for their respective regions. The latter, sponsored by the ruling African National Congress (ANC), was inaugurated by President Nelson Mandela. Just before, in August, a "Cuba Vive International Youth Festival" in Havana drew over 1,000 participants from 67 countries.

There had also been a spate of Cuban "solidarity" meetings in 1992, led off by an apparently never-exceeded 3,400-strong gathering in New York in January.[37] This was followed in April by another "first": the "First Latin America and Caribbean Meeting of Friendship and Solidarity with Cuba" in Havana. The latter had a mere 200 to 300 participants, but another meeting in Bonn in May was said to have brought together over 1,000 persons.[38] There was growth in the number of claimed Cuban-support organizations during the period between these two series of meetings. In mid-1992, the Cuban press reported over 800 "solidarity organizations" in some 93 countries;[39] in late 1995, the comparable figures were 1,500 organizations in 123 countries.[40]

What may be involved in this near-universal support for Cuba on the part of the Left is a possible recent attempt by the latter to come together with the other traditional purely communist ruling parties in China, Vietnam, Laos, and North Korea. The Cuban press noted that the Havana chiefs of mission for these four Asian nations plus Cambodia had gotten together at the Cuban celebration of the KWP's 50th anniversary in October 1995.[41] Then, in July 1996, PCC Politburo member Jose Ramon Balaguer visited these same four Asian countries just prior to leading the Cuban delegation to the Sao Paulo Forum meeting in San Salvador. This meeting was also attended by delegations from China, Vietnam, Laos, and North Korea. In the intervening period, as if to pick up on the ruling party solidarity theme, British KWP apologist Keith Bennett published an article lauding China, Cuba, North Korea, Vietnam, and Laos across the board and quoting Russia's North Korean fan Nina Andreyeva in calling for support to the five countries.[42] This was quite a new emphasis for Pyongyang's friends, but one the Cubans may have been able to bring about.

Cuban Leadership Beyond Latin America

Just as most of the traditional international communist fronts, consonant with the political changes experienced by their former Soviet and East European supporters, were retrenching and becoming less active, the Havana-based (and Cuban-controlled?) Organization of Solidarity of the People's of Africa, Asia, and Latin America (OSPAAAL) was enjoying a new lease on life. The first inkling we had of this was in the *Yearbook of International Organization: 1993-1994* notation that OSPAAAL had 27 full-time staffers at its headquarters. The *Links*-associated *Green Left Weekly* implied that these included representatives from Vietnam, Syria, North Korea, and Palestine representing Asia; from Congo, Guinea, South Africa, and Angola for Africa; and from Cuba, Chile, Puerto Rico, and the Dominican Republic for Latin America.[43]

Following this discovery, in November, 1994, just prior to the "First World Solidarity Conference with Cuba," and probably making use of many of the same delegates, OSPAAAL held an international "Encounter of the Right of Peoples to Social Development" in the same city, an event that claimed over 1,000 delegates from over 50 countries.[44] This was followed by the April, 1995, announcement that the organization's *Tricontinental* magazine would be published again after a four-year hiatus. The start-up was made possible by financial support from "Italian revolutionaries."[45] Finally, in January, 1996, OSPAAAL was reported to have celebrated its 30th anniversary with a Havana meeting attended by 180 representatives from 41 countries and six international organizations.[46]

As for worldwide fronts, the Cubans hosted the 14th World Youth Festival in July-August 1997. Though not reaching previous levels (see above), this festival did manage to bring together over 12,000 delegates from 132 countries[47] in what was certainly the most impressive such meeting of the post-1990 era. (The World Youth Festivals have traditionally been co-sponsored by the World Federation of Democratic Youth, the international Union of Students, and the host-country's affiliates of each.) The Festival was followed almost immediately (August 6-7) by yet another Havana meetimg, an "International Conference of Trade Unions Against Globalization and Neocolonialism of Economy." Though sponsored solely by the Central Organization of Cuban Trade Unions (CTC), it was attended by between 1,000 and 1,300 delegates from some 400 trade unions in 61 countries and was regarded as important enough by the World Federation of Trade Unions to have its secretary general lead its delegation thereto and have over half of its *Flashes*, No. 14/97, devoted to it.[48]

As for more strictly party affairs, the Cuban Communist Party sponsored a conference entitled "Socialism Looks Toward the XXIst Century" in October 1997. The latter had participants from 97 communist and pro-communist parties from 48 countries[49] and was described by the CPI-M's *People's Democracy* of November 9, 1997, as a larger successor to the May 1993 Karl Marx seminar in Calcutta (see above). (The latter had only 22 delegations from 20 countries.[50]) Clearly, the Cubans in 1997 were cashing in on their aforenoted near-universal acceptability among the world's far Leftist forces.

Notes

1. Richard F. Staar (ed.), 1991 Yearbook on International Communist Affairs (Stanford: Hoover Institution, 1991), p. 55, quoting *Correio Brasiliense*, July 5, 1990.

2. Ibid., 1990, p. 56, quoting *O Estado de Sao Paulo*, June 11, 1989, regarding Lula's statement on Chinese repression.

3. *New York Times*, July 29, 1996.

4. Stephen Marks, "Montevideo's Sao Paulo Forum," *Links* (Broadway, NSW, Australia), January-April 1996, p. 11.

5. *El Diario de Hoy* (San Salvador), July 27, 1996.

6. *The Militant* (New York), April 23, 1993, June 12, 1995, and September 2, 1996.

7. Alfonso Moro, "Where is the Latin American Left Heading?," *International Viewpoint* (Paris), July 20, 1995, p. 4.

8. Braulio Moro Interview, *International Viewpoint* (Paris), op. cit., pp. 12-13.

9. *New Age* (New Delhi), September 5, 1993.

10. "The Latin American Left in the 90's," *Links* (Broadway, NSW, Australia), April-June 1994, pp. 5, 10-11.

11. *Pyongyang Times*, August 1, 1992.

12. *Chen Ming* (Hongkong), January 1, 1994 (FBIS, January 25, 1994).

13. *L'Humanite* (Paris), December 19, 1990, September 14, 1991, September 12, 1992, September 11, 1993, January 26, 1994, September 10, 1994, September 16, 1995.

14. Brian Weinstein, "Haiti," in Richard F. Staar, op. cit., 1991, p. 94.

15. *The Militant* (New York), February 14, 1994.

16. Ibid.

17. Ibid., August 23, 1993, and February 14, 1994.

18. Stephen Marks, op. cit., p. 5.

19. William Ratliff, "Introduction: the Americas," Richard F. Staar (ed.), op. cit., 1990, p. 41.

20. *Granma International* (Havana), March 11, 1990; Douglas W. Payne, "Guyana," Richard F. Staar (ed.), op. cit., 1991, p. 92.

21. *Granma International* (Havana), March 11, 1990; *Granma* (Havana), February 3, 1990.

22. *El Dia* (Mexico City), November 30, 1990; *Barricada* (Managua) July 22, 1991.

23. William Ratliff, "Introduction: the Americas," Richard F. Staar (ed.), op. cit., 1991, p. 45.

24. *Granma International* (Havana), January 26, 1992.

25. Colin M. MacLachlan, "Mexico," Richard F. Staar (ed.), op. cit., 1991, p. 102.

26. *El Da* (Mexico City), November 29 and 30, 1990.

27. *People's Democracy* (New Delhi), June 13, 1993.

28. Pyongyang, KCNA, April 20, 1995 (FBIS, April 20, 1995).

29. *The People's Korea* (Tokyo), April 4, 1992.

30. G. H. Andersen, "Communist Forces Are Regrouping," *SPA News*

(Aukland), November 1992, p. 6.

31. Ibid., p. 7; *El Da* (Mexico City).

32. *Granma* (Havana), July 24, 1993.

33. *People's Democracy* (New Delhi), December 18, 1994.

34. Ibid., September 21, 1997.

35. *Granma International* (Havana), November 30 and December 7, 1994.

36. *International Viewpoint* (Paris), March 1995, pp. 8, 13.

37. *Granma International* (Havana), February 2, 1992.

38. *Trabajadores* (Havana), April 13, 1992; *Granma* (Havana), May 26, 1992.

39. *Granma International* (Havana), June 14, 1992.

40. Ibid., December 20, 1995.

41. *Granma* (Havana), October 6, 1995.

42. *The New Worker* (London), December 1, 1995.

43. *Green Left Weekly* (Broadway, NSW, Australia), March 1, 1995.

44. *Granma* (Havana), November 19, 1994; *Peace Courier* (Helsinki), November 12, 1994.

45. *Granma International* (Havana), April 19, 1995; *Green Left Weekly* (Broadway, NSW, Australia), March 1, 1995.

46. *Pyongyang Times*, January 27, 1996; *Granma International* (Havana), January 31, 1996.

47. *The Militant* (New York), August 25, 1997.

48. *Flashes* (Prague), Nos. 14 and 15-16, 1997; *Granma International* (Havana), August 17, 1997.

49. *Granma International* (Havana), November 2, 1997; *People's Democracy* (New Delhi), November 9, 1997.

50. Ibid., May 9, June 13, and June 27, 1993.

Chapter 6

Is a Future Comintern
Being Created?

Amorphous Worldwide System

We have surveyed the complexes formed by the 235 signers of the 1992 North Korean Pyongyang Declaration (PD), the some 250 participants in the French Communist Party (PCF)-sponsored conferences during 1990-1997, the 20 parties represented on the staff of *Links* magazine (founded in 1994), and certain organizational manifestations found in Latin America during this same 1990-1997 period. We found that there was an overlap (common membership) in some 50 cases between the two largest systems—the PD and PCF conferences—and that three of these "overlappers" also serve on the staff of *Links*.

The Sao Paulo Forum, we found, is by far the most significant of the Latin American groups covered here. Of the six dominant parties in the Forum, two are in this small PD-PCF conference-Links staff "overlap" group. Two or three of the others are in the PCF conference system only; the sixth is associated with the PD. Of the 17 other, less-connected *Links* parties, five (consisting of one, possibly two more of the Sao Paulo Forum's "big six," and three of its non-Latin American observers) are participants of the PCF conference system only.

Thus, we find that there is a substantial number of interlocking relationships binding this amorphous system together. There is also a large number of parties that are members of one group only and, therefore, left in a "dangling" status, as among the approximately 112 members of the Sao Paulo Forum. Whereas the PD signers and PCF conferees tend toward the Left and Right poles of the far Left spectrum, respectively, the situation is complicated by the fact that the Socialist International (SI), which generally stands outside and to the Right of this whole larger system, now has as full members one of the PD-signing-only parties (February Revolutionary Party of Paraguay) and three PD-PCF "overlappers" (Socialist Party of Chile, Progressive Socialist Party of Lebanon, and Sandinist National Liberation Front [FSLN] of Nicaragua) as well as, more predictably, some ten in the PCF-conference-only category. The FSLN and the Mexican Revolutionary Democratic Party (PRD), the only two of the Sao Paulo Forum's "big six" having SI membership, achieved this status only in late 1996. The FSLN is also the only SI member on the *Links* staff. This means that *all* the far Left systems we have chosen to examine here are, at least in a small way, linked to the SI.

Relatively Tight Regional Organizations of Relatively Successful Left Parties

The Sao Paulo Forum has a Working Group (SPFWG) dominated by six parties. All of these except the ruling Cuban Communist Party (PCC) are viable Opposition parties operating within a parliamentary democratic framework in their respective countries. This has led a small and abjectly pro-Cuban party to picture the "revolutionary" Cubans pitted against the others, which have allegedly "sold out" to the bourgeois political system.[1] That this picture is skewed can be seen in the facts that Castro himself has endorsed the parliamentary way for non-Cuban Latin American Leftists at this stage of their (and their countries') development while at the same time the sometimes critical *Links* has acknowledged that Cuba is *the* inspiration for *all* of the Forum.[2] This parliamentary orientation, plus the Forum's buying of the Chinese-espoused line of the "North-South" struggle (replacing the "East -West" one), would seem to place the Forum in the Center of the Latin American far Left. The U.S., of course, remains the "main enemy."

This posture at least goes against the "East-West" struggle emphasized by the PD, which was *signed by half* of the "big six": the FSLN, the

Farabundo Marti National Liberation Front (FMLN) of El Salvador, and the Broad Front (FA) of Uruguay. This may be a cause of underlying tension, as might the historical association of Eurocommunism with the Mexican PRD, Trotskyism with the Brazilian Workers' Party (PT), and pro-Moscow "main-line" communism with the other four. Note that both the Chinese and North Koreans sent observers to the 1996 Forum.

The Forum receives enthusiastic support and publicity from *Links* magazine, which we previously identified as a kind of Centrist institution within the whole worldwide Left spectrum. This is consistent with the fact that the PT, FMLN, FSLN, and possibly the PCC have representatives on the *Links* staff. (It is not clear to what extent the Cubans on *Links* represent the PCC.) It is also consistent with the fact that the participation of the *Links*-founder Democratic Socialist Party (DSP) of Australia as a Forum observer is its only activity we have noted in these other far Left complexes, other than attendance at the December 1996 PCF Congress.

On the other hand, the Forum suffers from a notable lack of support in the English-speaking Caribbean. This is not surprising in that that area has had an inexplicably high number of PD signers who have not participated in the PCF system (see Chapter 2). Though the Labor Party of Dominica had been put on the SPFWG in 1994, neither it nor any other English-speaking Caribbean party was represented at the 1995 or 1996 Fora.[3]

Two other recent SPFWG cooptees, both ruling parties with less than full member status in the SI—the Lavalas Political Organization of Haiti and the Democratic Revolutionary Party of Panama—also missed at least the 1995 Forum. Thus, what we are talking about as a "relatively tight regional organization of relatively successful Left parties" is not the whole Working Group but its "big six" core, plus possibly its constituent Communist Party of Guadeloupe (PCG), in light of the hyperactivity of its PCF parent.

The Confederal European United Left (CEUL) is another relatively cohesive far Left regional grouping of relative "winners," parties having received at least five per cent of the electoral vote in their respective countries necessary for representation in the European Parliament. Again somewhat of a "mixed bag," although more uniformly communist than the "big six" described above, this 32-member, eight party group consists of the Portuguese Communist Party (PCP)-dominated Unified Democratic Coalition (CDU) (3 seats) and the Communist Party of Greece (KKE)(2 seats) on the relatively "Stalinist" Left; the Refoundation Italian Communist Party (RPCI)(5 seats) in the Left-Center (see below); the PCF (7 seats) in the Right Center; and the Spanish Communist Party (PCE)-

dominated United Left (IU)(9 seats), the Left Party (VP) of Sweden (3 seats), Progressive Left Coalition (*Synaspismos*) of Greece (2 seats), and the Left Alliance (VL) of Finland (1 seat) on the Eurocommunist Right. In spite of this variation, the situation is more clear-cut here than in the case of the Sao Paulo Forum's "big six," for none are members of the SI (which has its own Europarliament bloc) and none signed the PD.

The fact that the PCF seemed to have captured the ideological Center here—between the two extremes, but leaning toward the more powerful Right—plus the facts of its Number 2 strength position and its overall vitality as communist organizer (see Chapter 3 and below) seemed to make it inevitable that it would emerge as leader of this group. This seems to have been borne out in that it was the PCF that called the aforenoted (Chapter 3) and well-publicized and well-attended Paris conference on unemployment in May 1996. At this conference, these very eight parties plus seven others furnished the featured speakers. One of these others— the Socialist People's Party (SF), formerly a member of one of two communist Europarliament blocs —now has one seat in the 29-member Green Group bloc.

Five of the others fell short of the requisite five percent vote but are assumed nevertheless to have been somewhat successful far Left groups in their respective countries: Party of Democratic Socialism (PDS) of Germany, Initiative of Catalonia, Independent Left of Ireland, Left Socialist Party (SV) of Norway, and Movement of United Communists of Italy (a split from the RPCI).

A seventh speaker was a British Labourite, but he appears to have been there solely in his expert capacity as a member of the Europarlia- ment's Commission on Employment. However, the same person turned up with another Labourite Europarliamentarian at the PCF's December 1996 Congress, but in what capacity is not known. The other six here appear to have been a kind of "second string" mobilized for action by the PCF, with the PDS being the most interesting from our standpoint. The successor to the formerly ruling Socialist Unity Party (SED) of (East) Germany—it just missed getting the requisite five percent—had been noted above (Chapter 3) as having an especially close relationship with the PCF, and was elevated to the *Links* Editorial Board in 1996.

The CEUL and its extension noted above appear especially successful when compared to other far Left efforts in Europe during the 1990-1996 period. The minuscule Communist Party of Bulgaria appears to have enlisted some other 16-28 parties of a PD-North Korean orientation (reports vary) in an abortive attempt to set up a new "Comintern" in Sofia in early November 1995;[4] nothing further has been heard of this.

Self-styled "New Left" efforts in Europe also seem to have evaporated. An "Assembly of the European Left" had been held in July, 1993, in Paris involving the RCPI, PDS, the Trotskyist Revolutionary Communist League of France, the Fourth International *per se*, and the Left wing of the British Labour Party—basically the *Links* contingent for Western Europe—but *Links* carried no further information on the then-projected follow up conference in 1994.[5]

A more lasting movement appears to have been a New European Left Forum, apparently initiated by the Spanish IU, involving five other of the CEUL parties (unspecified): Green Left of the Netherlands, the Workers' Party (PO), and Democratic Left (Right wing split from PO) of Ireland, "the Scandinavian parties," and others. The group was allegedly meeting twice a year at least from November 1991 to March 1995, but again, no follow-up information was provided by *Links*, even though the aforenoted story came from its sister *Green Left Weekly* (of March 22, 1995).

"Magnet Parties"

The three PD-*Links*-PCF conference "overlappers"—the FSLN, the South African Communist Party (SACP), and the FMLN—each came fully into a parliamentary-democratic governmental system only in the early 1990s. The FSLN did so by accepting defeat in the 1990 elections and thereby becoming Nicaragua's chief Opposition party. Earlier, it had mitigated its semi-authoritarian rule by giving in under external pressure and holding free elections, boycotted by the then main Opposition elements in 1984. An agreement in 1989 made it possible for full Opposition participation in the then forthcoming elections.

Similarly, in El Salvador, the FMLN, by giving up its armed struggle against the government in 1991, paved the way for its becoming a legal political party the following year. It emerged from the early 1994 elections as the country's main Opposition force. The South African government's lifting of the ban on the SACP and the larger and broader African National Congress (ANC) of which it was a part, again, in 1990, paved the way for the 1994 elections, in which the SACP became a de facto junior partner in an ANC-dominated government.

The participation of the FSLN, FMLN, and CPSA in their respective countries' democratic processes squares with their participation in the publication of *Links* magazine, with its openly-stated opposition to political authoritarianism (see Chapter 4). Their 1992 signature of the PD indicates, however, that they at least pay lip service to working for the eventual triumph of communist-style "socialism" and combatting U.S.-led "imperialism." Continued participation of the FSLN and FMLN in the Sao Paulo Forum at least indicates an intention on their part to follow this latter emphasis (in spite of the aforenoted upgrading of the FSLN's status in the Sl in 1996). Collectively, these three parties, as much as any others, set the tone for the internationally active far Left at present: tolerance for and use of parliamentary democracy where it exists to achieve some sort of Marxist regime at home while opposing, by any means practicable, U.S. "imperialism" abroad. By participating in the various international networks described here, moreover, these three show a willingness to work with a very broad spectrum of the far Left to help achieve their objectives.

The unifying function of the Cuban Communist Party (PCC) within the far Left also should be emphasized again. First, it has been notable in trying to bring the other old-line, traditionally ruling communist parties— in China, Laos, North Korea, and Vietnam—into the mainstream of the Latin American far Left. This was graphically illustrated when Jose Balaguer visited these four countries just prior to leading the Cuban delegation to the 1996 Sao Paulo Forum meeting in San Salvador and when all four (apparently for the first time) sent delegations to this meeting.

Second, the universal appeal of the Cubans among the far Left could be seen when, at the 1994 Havana "First World Solidarity Conference with Cuba," the most notable traveling leaders of both the PCF (Georges Marchais) and Korean Workers' Party (KWP) (Hwang Jang-yop) appeared, as did representatives from other Sao Paulo Forum "big six" and *Links* staff parties. The latter included a member of the Trotskyist Fourth International *per se*, but no one specifically representing the SI attended.[6] The SI is, of course, not far Left. The sponsoring of regional follow-up conferences in 1995 by the ANC in Johannesburg and the Communist Party of India-Marxist (CPI/M) in Calcutta merely emphasized the strong links these two important parties have traditionally maintained with Havana. For example, Castro was the "hit" at ANC President Mandela's 1994 inauguration as his country's president. CPI/M Secretary General H. S. Surjeet—"Cuba's best friend in India"—attended the Sao Paulo Forum apparently only when it was held in Havana in 1993.

The PCF and RPCI might be considered in tandem, since they both appear to occupy Center positions within the CEUL (see above), but complement each other as the former veers Rightward and the latter

Leftward. The RPCI's December 1996 Congress (with about 100 attendees, second only in number of foreign delegations to those of the PCF in this period) had a roughly 70 party overlap with the PCF's that same month, including each other, the other six CEUL parties, the other major "Free World" parties (in Cyprus, India, Japan, and South Africa), five of the Sao Paulo Forum's "big six" (all except the Uruguayan FA), and the Communist Parties of China, Russia (CP-RF), North Korea (KWP), and Vietnam[7]

The notable parties attending only the RPCI Congress tended to be on the far left: e.g., the ruling parties of Syria (Baath) and Serbia (Socialist) and miniscule PD signers from Russia, Slovokia, and Yugoslovia. The bulk of the PCF Congress-only attendees were from Africa, many with dubious Marxist credentials. Also, it was ironic that though the RPCI, not the PCF, participates directly in *Links*, it was only the latter's Congress that hosted the Australian DSP and American CoC, the two largest contributors to the magazine.

Aside from the cases of the extremely Left (and usually minuscule) parties treated herein, the appeal of the KWP and the bankrupt country it runs remains a mystery. Perhaps it is admiration of will power, and even ruthlessness, that gets even some relatively conservative African governments to take lessens from the KWP in "party building."

Notes

1. *The Militant* (New York), June 12, 1995, and September 2, 1996.

2. *New Age* (New Delhi), September 5, 1993; Stephen Marks, "Montevideo's Sao Paulo Forum," *Links* (Broadway, NSW, Australia). January-April 1995, p. 11.

3. *The Militant* (New York), June 12, 1995, and September 2, 1996.

4. *Kontinent* (Sofia), November 6, 1995 (Foreign Broadcast Information Service, November 9, 1995); *Le Figaro* (Paris), November 9, 1995.

5. "International Workers' Movement News," *Links* (Broadway, NSW, Australia), April-June 1994, p. 127.

6. *International Viewpoint* (Paris), March 8, 1995, p.13.

7. *Liberazione* (Rome), December 13, 1996.

Appendix I

The Pyongyang Declaration[1]

[*Leaders and delegates of communist workers' parties and other political parties aspiring after socialism, who came to Pyongyang to participate in the celebration of the 80th birthday of President Kim Il-song, had multilateral and bilateral contacts while staying in Pyongyang.*

Delegations of communist and workers' parties and other political parties aspiring after socialism decided to adopt a Pyongyang Declaration reflecting the firm will to defend and advance the cause of socialism and, to this end, had contacts with other progressive political parties which could not send delegates to Pyongyang.

The Pyongyang Declaration was signed by delegates of 70 parties of the world, including 48 party leaders as of April 20 this year (1992).

Follows the full text of the Pyongyang Declaration titled "Let Us Defend and Advance the Socialist Cause."]

The representatives of political parties from different countries of the world who are striving for the victory of socialism publish this declaration with a firm conviction to defend and advance the socialist cause.

Ours is an era of independence and the socialist cause is a sacred one aimed at realizing the independence of the popular masses.

Socialism suffered a setback in some countries in recent years. As a consequence of this, the imperialists and reactionaries are claiming that socialism has "come to an end." This is nothing but a sophistry to beautify and embellish capitalism and patronize the old order.

The setback of socialism and the revival of capitalism in some countries is causing a great loss to the achievement of socialist cause, but it can never be interpreted as the denial of the superiority of socialism and, of the reactionary character of capitalism.

Socialism has long been the ideal of mankind and it represents the future of mankind.

Socialist society is, in essence, a genuine society for the people where the popular masses are the masters of everything and everything serves them.

But the capitalist society is an unfair one where "the rich get ever richer and the poor poorer." In this society money decides everything, exploitation of man by man predominates and a handful of exploiter classes lords it over. It is inevitably accompanied by political non-rights, unemployment, poverty, drugs, crimes and other kinds of all social evils which trample the human dignity underfoot.

Only socialism can eliminate domination, subjugation and social inequality of all manners and ensure the people substantial freedom, equality, true democracy and human rights.

The popular masses have long carried on an arduous struggle for the victory of socialism and shed much blood in this course.

The past of socialism is an untrodden one and, therefore, the advance of socialism is inevitably accompanied by trials and difficulties.

One of the reasons for the unsuccessful construction of socialism in some countries is that they failed to build a social structure conforming to the fundamental requirements of the popular masses and build socialism suited to the demand of the theory of scientific socialism.

The guarantee for the advance of a socialist society lies in that the popular masses become the genuine masters of the society.

Such a society makes a triumphant advance—this is a truth and reality proved by theory and practice.

The parties and progressive mankind aspiring after socialism have drawn a very precious lesson therefrom.

In order to defend and advance the socialist cause individual parties should firmly maintain independence and firmly build up their own forces.

The socialist movement is an independent one. Socialism is carved out and built with a country or national state as a unit. The socialist cause in each country should be fulfilled on the responsibility of the party and people of that country.

Each party should work out lines of policies which tally with the actual situation of the country where it is active and with the demands of its people and implement them by relying on the popular masses.

It should not abandon its revolutionary principles at any time and under any circumstances but uplift the banner of socialism.

The socialist cause is a national one and, at the same time, a common cause of mankind.

All parties should cement the ties of comradely unity, cooperation and solidarity among themselves on the principle of independence and equality.

International solidarity is essential to the struggle for socialism.

Now that the imperialists and reactionaries are attacking socialism and people in an international collusion, the parties which are building socialism or aspiring after it should defend and advance socialism on an international scale and strengthen mutual support and solidarity in their efforts for social justice, democracy, the right to existence and peace against imperialist domination, subjugation by capital and neo-colonialism.

This is an international duty incumbent upon all parties and progressive forces for socialism and an undertaking for their own cause.

We will advance under the unfurled banner of socialism in firm unity with all progressive political parties, organizations and peoples of the world who are striving to defend socialism against capitalism and imperialism.

Let us all fight it out to open up the future of mankind with a firm conviction in the cause of socialism.

Final victory is on the part of the people fighting in unity for socialism.

The socialism cause shall not perish.

The Original 70 Signatories (in order listed)[2]

Legend:

      * Officially recognized by former Soviet Union as communist or "vanguard" party, 1988-90.

      # "Follow-on" to above such parties.

      @ Formerly recognized by Soviet Union as "revolutionary democratic" party or "liberation movement."

      ¢ Not listed in *Political Handbook of the World, 1992*

Asia

1. Workers' Party of Bangladesh
2. Bangladesh National Socialist Party
3. Progressive Party of the Working People of Cyprus *
4. Communist Party of India (Marxist) *
5. Communist Party of India *
6. Jordanian Communist Party *
7. Workers' Party of Korea*
8. National Socialist Party of Syria in Lebanon
9. Mongolian People's Revolutionary Party *
10. Nepalese Communist Party (united Marxist-Leninist) #
11. Nepalese Communist Party (united Centre) ¢
12. Nepal Workers and Peasants Party
13. Nepalese Communist Party (united) ¢
14. Sri Lanka Communist Party *
15. Arab Socialist Ba'ath Party (Syria) @
16. Socialist Party of Turkey

Europe

17. Communist Party of Albania
18. Communist Party of Bulgaria
19. Bulgarian Communist Party (Marxists)
20. Belgian Labour Party
21. Britannic Communist Party *¢
22. New Communist Party of Great Britain ¢
23. Danish Workers Party Common Cause
24. For Peace and Socialism Communist Forum of Denmark ¢
25. Communist Workers' Party of Finland

26. German Communist Party *
27. Hungarian Socialist Workers' Party
28. Communist Party of Ireland *
29. Movement for Peace and Socialism of Italy ¢
30. New Socialist Party of Romania ¢
31. Communist Party of Malta *
32. Norwegian Communist Party *
33. Polish League of Communists (proletariat) ¢
34. All-Union Bolshevik Communist Party (Russia)
35. Russian Communist Workers' Party #¢
36. Russian Socialist Workers' Party ¢
37. "Communists League" of Russia ¢
38. Spanish People's Communist Party *
39. Labour Party—Communists of Sweden *
40. League of Communists—Movement for Yugoslavia #

Americas

41. Communist Party of Argentina *
42. Barbados Workers' Party
43. Communist Party of Venezuela *
44. New Alternative of Venezuela
45. Progressive Labour Party of Bermuda
46. Bolivian Communist Party *
47. Brazilian Communist Party *
48. Caribbean National Movement
49. Communist Party of Chile *
50. Socialist Party of Chile
51. Communist Party of Colombia *
52. People's Party of Costa Rica *
53. Dominican Communist Party *
54. United Left Movement of Dominica ¢
55. Dominican Labour Party
56. Communist Party of Ecuador *
57. Maurice Bishop Patriotic Movement of Grenada
58. Communist Party of Martinique *
59. Popular Socialist Party of Mexico
60. Communist Party of Paraguay *
61. St. Kitts-Nevis Labour Party
62. National Democratic Party of Surinam

63. February 18 Movement of Trinidad and Tobago ¢
64. Communist Party of the United States (of America)*
65. Socialist Workers Party of America
66. Workers World Party of the United States ¢

Africa

67. Popular Liberation Movement of Angola *
68. South West Africa People's Organization of Namibia @
69. South African Communist Party *
70. People's Unity Party of Tunisia

Notes

---

1. Source for text and 70 signatories: *The People's Korea* (Tokyo),May 2-9, 1992.

2. *Pyongyang Times* (April 28, 1992) noted representatives of the following communist parties at Kim Il-sung's Pyongyang birthday celebrations which, nevertheless, did not sign the Declaration: Cambodia, China, Cuba, Laos, Portugal, and Vietnam.

Appendix II

Parties Recently Related to French and Korean Communists

French Communist Congress and Newspaper Festival Attendees, 1990 through 1997, and Pyongyang Declaration Signers, 1992 through 1997

Legend:

Parties:
Those parties mentioned in authoritative, Soviet-edited (A. Subbotin) and Czech-published (*Peace and Socialism*, 1988) *First Hand Information* are listed in ***bold italics***. Major successors to these parties are in normal *italics*. All cited from this source are identified as either communist or "vanguard revolutionary democratic" (near communist).

Activities:

<u>X</u>   Top participant at French communist meeting cited (president, secretary general, first secretary, or chief editor [in the case of newspaper festivals]).

X   Lesser-ranking participant in such a meeting.

(X)   Solely a Paris embassy representative (in the case of ruling parties); or, for Algeria, an unlabelled person in 1994 who had represented the PADS in 1993.

Source of the above: *L'Humanite* (Paris), December 19, 1990, September 14, 1991, September 12, 1992, September 11, 1993, January 26, 1994, February 1, 1994, September 10 and 13, 1994, September 16, 1995, September 17, 1996, December 20 and 21, 1996, and September 16, 1997.

*   188 known signers of Pyongyang Declaration (out of 235 claimed).

(*)   17 additional participants in meetings celebrating Pyongyang Declaration or supporting DPRK (Pyongyang Times, April 24 and May 1, 1993); except for Mongolia, MPRP, which signed and later renounced its signature; Socialist Party of Aoteoroa, which carried the Declaration in its News of November 1992, and the Party of Revolution of Benin and Amerindian Action Movement of Guyana, which made Kim Chong-il their honorary leader in late 1994 and late 1995, respectively -- probable signers. (Note that among known Declaration signers the People's League of Bangladesh made Kim Chong-il its honorary leader in late 1995 as did the Costa Rican People's Party and Grenadan Maurice Bishop Patriotic Movement in early 1996.)

Sources of the above: *Pyongyang Times*, April 28, 1992, through October 12, 1996; Pyongyang, KCNA, April 21, 1995 (FBIS, April 21 and 24, 1995), October 23, 1995 (FBIS, October 27, 1995), and November 4, 1995 (FBIS, November 8, 1995); *The People's Korea* (Tokyo), June 21 and October 28, 1995, March 2, 1996, April 26, 1997.

\#   Sole representative of its country at both January 1993 Congress of the Communist Party of Nepal/United Marxist-Leninist and May 1993 Marxism seminar sponsored by the Communist Party of India/Marxist (People's Democracy [New Delhi] February 7, May 9, 1993).

@   Sao Paulo Forum Working Group (The Militant [New York], August 23, 1993).

S   Full member of Socialist International; (S) Consultant or observer member thereof

COUNTRY Party	90 27th Con	91 Fes	92 Fes	93 Fes	94 28th Con	94 Fes	95 Fes	96 Fes	96 29th Con	97 Fes
AFGHANISTAN:										
Vatan (Fatherland) Party		X								
ALBANIA:										
Socialist Party (PSS)		X								X
Communist Party*										
ALGERIA:[1]										
Socialist Vanguard Party (PAGS) / Movement Etta-haddi	X	X	X	X		X̲		X	X	X
National Liberation Front (FLN)	X	X	X̲						X	
Party for Democracy and Socialism (PADS)				X	(X)	X	X	X	X	X
Rally for Culture and Democracy (RCD)								X	X̲	X
Assembly of Democratic Algerian Women (RAFD)										X
General Union of Algerian Workers (UGTA)									X	X
National Republican Alliance (ANR)									X	
Socialist Forces Front (FFS)									X	
Women Acting in Immigration and for Solidarity (?)(FAIS)									X	
ANGOLA:										
***Popular Movement for the Liberation of Angola (MPLA)*(S)**	(X)				X	(X)	X	X	X	

---

[1] In addition, *Algier republicain* sent delegations to the *L'Humanite* Festivals of 1991-92, 1994-95, 1997, and the Congresses of 1994 and 1996.

COUNTRY Party	90 27th Con	91 Fes	92 Fes	93 Fes	94 28th Con	94 Fes	95 Fes	96 Fes	96 29th Con	97 Fes
Party of Communists *										
Social Communist Party *										
ARGENTINA:										
Communist Party (PCA)*	X		X	X	X	X	<u>X</u>	X	X	X
May Place Association of Mothers									X	
Popular Insurgency Party*									X	
Revolutionary Workers Party (POR/PRT) (Trotskyist)*										
Revolutionary Party for the Independence and Socialism (of Argentina)*										
People's Movement*										
AUSTRALIA:										
Socialist Party*/*Communist Party (formed Oct 96)*	X			X	X	X				
Association for Communist Unity*										
Democratic Socialist Party									X	
AUSTRIA:										
Communist Party (KPO)	<u>X</u>	X	<u>X</u>	X	X	X	X		X	X
BAHAMAS:										
Vanguard Party*										
BAHRAIN:										
National Liberation Front	X			X			X	X		
Popular Front		X								
BANGLADESH:										

COUNTRY Party	90 27th Con	91 Fes	92 Fes	93 Fes	94 28th Con	94 Fes	95 Fes	96 Fes	96 29th Con	97 Fes
Popular Forum					X					
Awami League[2]	X									
People's League*										
Workers' Party*#										X
National Socialist Party*										
Socialist Party*										
Socialist Party of Workers and Peasants*										
Communist Party - Marx-ist-Leninist*										
BARBADOS:										
Workers' Party*										
Peoples Progressive Movement*										
BELARUS:										
Party of Communists (re-formed June 93?)*					X				X	
BELGIUM:										
Union of Communists (UCB)/PCB (Communist Party?)	X	X	X	X	X	X	X̲	X̲	X̲	X
Committee for Cancella-tion of Third World Debt (CADTM)									X	
OXFAM									X	
Labor Party (PTB)* (for-merly pro-Chinese; pre-sumably identical to										

---

[2] Though Awami means "People's," the currently ruling Awami League under President Sheikh Hasina Wajed is apparently different from the People's League under Chairman Garib Newaz.

Is the Comintern Coming Back?

COUNTRY Party	90 27th Con	91 Fes	92 Fes	93 Fes	94 28th Con	94 Fes	95 Fes	96 Fes	96 29th Con	97 Fes
Workers Party#)										
Communist Movement*										
BENIN:										
Communist Party								X		X
Party of Revolution (*)										
National Workers Party (*)										
BERMUDA:										
Progressive Labor Party*										
BOLIVIA:										
*Communist Party (PCB)**			X	X		X	X	X	X̲	
Free Bolivia Movement (MBL)@ (probably the "Liberal Bolivia Movement"* mentioned by Koreans)			X							
BOSNIA-HERZEGOVINA:										
Movement for Democratic Liberties (Serbian)							X			
Civic Forum									X	
BRAZIL:										
(Brazilian) Communist Party (PCB)/Popular Socialist Party (PPS)	X		X		X̲	X	X	X		
Workers Party (PT)@					X	X	X	X	X	X
Communist Party (of Brazil) (PCdoB) (formerly pro-Albanian)*					X				X	
October 8 Revolutionary Movement (MR8)*			X	X						
Communist Party (new)									X	

COUNTRY Party	90 27th Con	91 Fes	92 Fes	93 Fes	94 28th Con	94 Fes	95 Fes	96 Fes	96 29th Con	97 Fes
BULGARIA:										
Socialist Party (BSP) (formed April 90)	X		X		X					
Communist Party*										
Communist Party- Marxist*										
BURKINA FASO:										
Popular Front	X									
African Independence Party (PAI)	X				<u>X</u>					
Organization for Popular Democracy-Labor Movement (ODP-MT)							X			
Convention for Democracy and Progress (CDP)						X		X	X	
Democratic Revolutionary Youth Party (*)										
Socialist Party (*)										
BURUNDI:										
Democratic Front (FRODEBU)						X	X	X	X	X
CAMBODIA:										
People's Revolutionary Party (of Kampuchea) (PPRK) / People's Party (PPC) (formed Oct 91)	X				X				X	
CAMEROON:[3]										
People's Union (UPC) /	X	X		X	X	X	<u>X</u>	X		X

---

[3] *L'Avenir* (party, if any, unknown) sent a representative to the *L'Humanite* Festival of 1996.

COUNTRY / Party	90 27th Con	91 Fes	92 Fes	93 Fes	94 28th Con	94 Fes	95 Fes	96 Fes	96 29th Con	97 Fes
UPC-MANIDEM										
Social Democratic Front (S)					X			X		
CANADA:										
Six Nations Reservation						X				
Communist Party							X		X	
Communist Party (Marxist-Leninist) (formerly pro-Albanian)*										
Quebec Communist Party*										X
Quebec Party (PQ)									X	
CAPE VERDE:										
African Independence Party (PAICV) S	X								X	
CENTRAL AFRICAN REPUBLIC:										
Popular Patriotic Front					X					
Patriotic Front of Progress (FPP)					X	X	X	X	X	
CHAD:										
National Democratic Union (UND)		X		X	X		X	X	X	X
Union of Democratic Forces (UFD)			X							
CHILE:										
Movement of the Allenden Left (MIDA) (formed Oct 91)			X	X	X	X		X		
Communist Party (PCCh)*	X		X	X	X	X	X	X	X	
Socialist Party (PSCh)*S			X				X	X		X
Left Revolutionary Move-										

COUNTRY Party	90 27th Con	91 Fes	92 Fes	93 Fes	94 28th Con	94 Fes	95 Fes	96 Fes	96 29th Con	97 Fes
ment (MIR)*										
CHINA:										
Communist Party	X	X	X	X	X	X	X	X	X	X
COLOMBIA:										
Patriotic Union (same person as represented PCC in 93)			X						X̱	
Democratic Alliance -- April 19 Movement ([AD]M-19) (S)			X							
Communist Party (PCC)*	X			X	X	X̱	X		X̱	X
Revolutionary Workers Party (PRT)*										
COMOROS:										
Party of Labor and Progress (PCTP)	X			X	X	X				
Democratic Front									X	
CONGO:										
Party of Labor (PCT)	X						X		X	
Union of Progressive Forces (UFPC)				X						
Association of Friendship with the Peoples					X̱					
Union of African Progress and Social Democracy (PADS)									X	
Movement for Building a New Society*										
Socialist Party (*)										
Communist Party (*)										
African Socialist Movement (*)										

COUNTRY Party	90 27th Con	91 Fes	92 Fes	93 Fes	94 28th Con	94 Fes	95 Fes	96 Fes	96 29th Con	97 Fes
COSTA RICA:										
People's Party (PPC)* (Castroite)										
People's Vanguard Party (PVP) (*)										
CROATIA:										
Social-Democratic Action							X			
Dalmation Action							X		<u>X</u>	
CUBA:										
Communist Party@	X	X	X	X	X	X	X	X	X	X
CYPRUS:										
Progressive Party of the Working People (AKEL)*	X				X			X	X	
CZECH REPUBLIC:										
Communist Party of Bohemia and Moravia (KSCM) (formed Nov 90)	<u>X</u>	<u>X</u>	<u>X</u>	<u>X</u>	X	X		X	X	
Party of Communists (*)										
DENMARK:										
Communist Party (of Denmark) (DKP)	X		X		X		X		X	
Popular Socialist Party (PSP)			X						X	
Communist Party (in Denmark)					<u>X</u>				X	
Communist Forum*			X							
Red-Green Alliance									X	
Worker's Party, Common Cause*										

COUNTRY Party	90 27th Con	91 Fes	92 Fes	93 Fes	94 28th Con	94 Fes	95 Fes	96 Fes	96 29th Con	97 Fes
Marxist-Leninist Community Party (formerly pro-Albanian?)*										
DJIBOUTI:										
Front for the Restoration of Unity and Democracy (FRUD)					X		X	X		
DOMINICA:										
Labor Party*@(S)										
United Left Movement*										
People's Movement*										
DOMINICAN REPUBLIC:										
Communist Revolutionary Union					X					
*Communist Party (PCD)**		X	X	X		X	X	X		
Force of the Revolution								X		X
Revolutionary Party									X	
Resistance Force for People's Liberation*										
Communist Party (Marxist-Leninist)*										
ECUADOR:										
*Communist Party (PCE)**										
Broad Left Democratic Front (FADI)*										
Popular Democratic Movement (MPD)*										
Socialist Party (PSE)*										
EGYPT:										
Communist Party (HShM)	X	X	X̲	X̲	X	X	X		X	

COUNTRY Party	90 27th Con	91 Fes	92 Fes	93 Fes	94 28th Con	94 Fes	95 Fes	96 Fes	96 29th Con	97 Fes
Progressive Unionist Party									X	
Socialist People's Party									X	
EL SALVADOR:										
***Communist Party (PCE or PCES)*[4]**	X				X					
Farabundo Marti National Liberation Front (FMLN)*@	X		X	X	X	X	X	X	X	X
Revolutionary Party of Central American Working People (PRTC)*										
EQUATORIAL GUINEA:										
Convergence for Social Democracy (CPDS) (S)					X					
Convention for Popular and Social Democracy (CDPS)									X	
ERITREA:										
Liberation Front									X	
ESTONIA:										
Democratic Party of Labor					<u>X</u>				<u>X</u>	
ETHIOPIA:										
Workers' Party (successor dissolved May 91)	X									
FINLAND:										
Left Alliance (VL)	X				X				X	
Communist Party - Unity (SKP-Y)		<u>X</u>			<u>X</u>	X			X	<u>X</u>
Communist Workers Party										

---

[4] The PCES dissolved into the FMLN in or about August 1995.

COUNTRY Party	90 27th Con	91 Fes	92 Fes	93 Fes	94 28th Con	94 Fes	95 Fes	96 Fes	96 29th Con	97 Fes
(KTP)*										
For Peace and Socialism - Communist Workers Party*										
FRANCE:										
Communist Party (PCF)	X	X	X	X	X	X	X	X	X	X
GABON:										
National Relief Movement (MORENA)	X									
Party for Progress (PGP) (S)	X		X	X					X	X
Democratic Forum				X						
National Assembly of Woodcutters (RNB)					X	X	X		X	X
FDR (expansion unknown; possibly Revolutionary Democratic Front)					X					
GERMANY:										
Party of Democratic Socialism (formed Feb 90)	X	X	X	X	X	X		X		X
*Communist Party (DKP)**	X	X	X	X	X	X	X	X	X	X
Fredrich-Ebert Stiftung Foundation									X	
GREAT BRITAIN:										
Communist Party (of Great Britain) / Democratic Left (latter formed Nov 91)	X				X				X	
Socialist Movement					X	±[5]				

---

[5] The newspaper *Liberation* represented here is possibly the organ of the Socialist Movement.

COUNTRY / Party	90 27th Con	91 Fes	92 Fes	93 Fes	94 28th Con	94 Fes	95 Fes	96 Fes	96 29th Con	97 Fes
Communist Party (of Britain)* (formed 1988)		X	X	X	X	X	X	X	X	
Socialist Workers Party									X	
New Communist Party (of Great Britain)*										
Revolutionary Communist Party (Marxist Leninist)* (formerly pro-Albanian)										
GREECE:										
Communist Party (KKE)	X	X	X	X	X	X	X	X	X	X
Coalition of Left and Progress (formed June 92)				X	X	X	X	X	X	X
Panhellenic Socialist Movement (PASOK) S									X	X
GRENADA:										
Maurice Bishop Patriotic Movement*										
GUADELOUPE:										
***Communist Party**@**	X	X	X	X	X	X	X	X	X	X
GUATEMALA:										
National Revolutionary Union (URNG)*@	X				X					
GUINEA:										
Democratic Party of Guinea - African Democratic Rally (PDG-RDA)									X	X
GUYANA:										
People's Progressive Party	X									
Labor Party*										
People's Democratic Movement*										

COUNTRY Party	90 27th Con	91 Fes	92 Fes	93 Fes	94 28th Con	94 Fes	95 Fes	96 Fes	96 29th Con	97 Fes
United Force Party*										
United Workers Party*										
National Movement for Authentic Independence*										
Amerindian Action Movement (*)										
GUYANE:										
Socialist Party (PSG)					X					
Communist Party										X
HAITI:										
Unified Party of Haitian Communists (PUCH)	X		X	X						
Lavallas Political Organization@(S)				X					X	
National Popularist Front						X̲				
HONDURAS:										
Party for Transformation*										
Movement for Unity of the People's Revolution*										
HUNGARY:[6]										
Socialist Party (MSP) (formed Oct 89) S						X				
Socialist Workers' Party (HSWP or MSZMP; a small Left splinter of party formerly having this name) / Labor Party*	X̲	X̲	X	X	X̲	X̲	X	X	X	
Left Alternative									X	

---

[6] The formerly Hungarian Socialist Workers' Party (ruling prior to October 1989), now "non-party" *Nepszabadsag*, sent its Paris representatives to the *L'Humanite* Festivals of 1994, 1996, and 1997.

COUNTRY / Party	90 27th Con	91 Fes	92 Fes	93 Fes	94 28th Con	94 Fes	95 Fes	96 Fes	96 29th Con	97 Fes
INDIA:										
Janata Dal (People's Party) (S)					X̲					
Congress					X̲					
Communist Party (CPI) *	X	X	X	X	X̲	X	X	X	X	X
Communist Party/Marxist (CPI-M) *	X		X		X	X			X	
Revolutionary Socialist Party*										
IRAN:										
Tudeh (Masses) Party	X	X		X		X	X	X	X	
People's Fedayeen Organization		X								
Majority Fedayeen Organization				X		X		X	X	X
Democratic Party of (Iranian) Kurdistan (S)					X	X	X	X	X	
IRAQ:										
Communist Party	X		X		X̲	X	X	X	X	X
Democratic Party of (Iraqi) Kurdistan	X				X	X	X			X
Patriotic Union of Kurdistan					X					
IRELAND:										
Sinn Fein (Ourselves Alone)		X				X	X	X		X
Democratic Left				X		X	X	X	X	X
Communist Party *	X				X					
Workers Party*	X		X		X				X	
ISRAEL:										
Communist Party	X̲				X		X	X	X	X

COUNTRY Party	90 27th Con	91 Fes	92 Fes	93 Fes	94 28th Con	94 Fes	95 Fes	96 Fes	96 29th Con	97 Fes
(RAKAH)										
Meretz (Vitality)					X				X	
ITALY:										
Communist Party (PCI) / Democratic Party of the Left (PDS) S	X		X	X	X	X̲				
Refoundation Italian Communist Party (PCRI)			X	X	X	X	X	X	X	X
Movement of Unitary Communists									X	
Movement for Peace and Socialism*										
IVORY COAST:										
Popular Front (FPI) S	X	X			X	X			X	
Workers Party (PIT)				X	X	X	X		X	
Democratic Party - RDA									X	
JAPAN:										
Communist Party (JCP)	X	X	X	X	X	X	X	X	X	X
JORDAN:										
Communist Party*	X		X		X̲					
Democratic Socialist Party*					X				X	
Democratic Party for Progress*										
Democratic Peoples Unity Party*										
Arab Progressive Ba'ath Party*										
National Democratic Vanguard Movement*										
National Action Front*										

COUNTRY Party	90 27th Con	91 Fes	92 Fes	93 Fes	94 28th Con	94 Fes	95 Fes	96 Fes	96 29th Con	97 Fes
Arab Peoples Liberation Movement*										
United Organization of the Arab Socialist Ba'ath Party*										
Arab Democratic Party*										
Peoples Revolutionary Party*										
Peoples Democratic Party*										
KAZAKHSTAN:										
Socialist Party*					X					
KOREA (NORTH, DPRK):										
Workers' Party (KWP)*#	X	X			X	(X)	X	(X)	X	
KOREA (SOUTH, ROK):										
National Democratic Front of South Korea(*)										
LAOS:										
People's Revolutionary Party (PPRL)	X		(X)		(X)	(X)	X		(X)	
LEBANON:										
Communist Party*	X		X		X	X̲	X	X	X̲	X
Progressive Socialist Party*S	X									
Regional Committee of the Arab Socialist Ba'ath*										
National Socialist Party of Syria in Lebanon*										
LUXEMBOURG:										
Communist Party	X		X	X	X	X	X		X̲	

COUNTRY / Party	90 27th Con	91 Fes	92 Fes	93 Fes	94 28th Con	94 Fes	95 Fes	96 Fes	96 29th Con	97 Fes
MADAGASCAR:										
Congress Party for Madagascar Independence (AKFM)	X				<u>X</u>	<u>X</u>	<u>X</u>	X		
Monima Socialist Organization*										
Democratic Committee for Supporting the Socialist Revolutionary Charter*										
Vanguard of the Revolution*										
Socialist Progressive Party*										
Militant Party for Equality*										
United Party for Struggle*										
New Party for the Renaissance (*)										
Party for the Defense of the Rights of the Masses (*)										
Patriotic Movement of Workers (*)										
MALI:										
Party of Revolution and Democracy (PMRD)	X									
Alliance for Democracy -- African Party for Solidarity and Justice (ADEMA) (S)					<u>X</u>	<u>X</u>			X	
MIRIA							<u>X</u>	X	X	
African Democratic Rally -- Sudanese Union (US-RDA) (*)					X	X	X	X	X	

COUNTRY Party	90 27th Con	91 Fes	92 Fes	93 Fes	94 28th Con	94 Fes	95 Fes	96 Fes	96 29th Con	97 Fes
MALTA:										
Communist Party*										
MARTINIQUE:										
Communist Party*	X	X̲	X̲	X	X̲	X	X	X̲	X̲	X̲
MAURETANIA:										
African Liberation Forces (FLAM)							X	X̲	X	
MAURITIUS:										
Communist Party*			X̲		X	X				
MEXICO:										
Revolutionary Democratic Party (PRD)@S					X̲				X̲	X
Popular Socialist Party (PPS)*					X					
Zapatista National Liberation Front (FZLN)									X	
Workers Party*										
MONGOLIA:										
People's Revolutionary Party (MPRP) (*)	X		X̲							
MOROCCO:										
Party of Progress and Socialism (PPS)*	X	X	X	X	X	X	X	X	X	X
Democratic and Popular Action Organization (OADP)	X								X	
Istiqlal (Independence) Party			X̲	X		X	X̲			
Democratic Socialist Vanguard Party (PADS)				X	X	X		X	X	

COUNTRY Party	90 27th Con	91 Fes	92 Fes	93 Fes	94 28th Con	94 Fes	95 Fes	96 Fes	96 29th Con	97 Fes
Socialist Union of Popular Forces (USFP) S					X				X	
Moroccan Unionist Movement							X	X		X
Democratic Alliance									X	
MOZAMBIQUE:										
Liberation Front (FRELIMO) (S)	X				(X)	(X)			X	
NAMIBIA:										
Southwest Africa People's Organization (SWAPO)*	X				(X)	(X)			X	
NEPAL:										
Communist Party / United Marxist-Leninist (CPN/UML)#									X	
Communist Party / United Center*										
Workers and Peasants Party*										
Communist Party/United*										
NETHERLANDS:										
Communist Party (CPN) / PCH (expansion un-known)? / New Communist Party (NPCN)			X	X	<u>X</u>	X				
Socialist Party								X	X	X
NEW CALEDONIA:										
Kanak Socialist National Liberation Front (FLNKS)	X									X
Kanak and Exploited Workers Union (USTKE)				X						

Country / Party	90 27th Con	91 Fes	92 Fes	93 Fes	94 28th Con	94 Fes	95 Fes	96 Fes	96 29th Con	97 Fes
NEW ZEALAND:										
Socialist Unity Party									X	
Socialist Party of Aoteoroa (*)										
NICARAGUA:										
Sandinista National Liberation Front (FSLN) *@S	X	X	X	X	X	X	X	X	X	X
Communist Party (formerly Trotskyist)*										
Marxist-Leninist Popular Action Movement*										
NIGER:										
Party for Democracy and Socialism (PNDS) (S)				X	X	X	X		X	
Revolutionary Organization for New Democracy									X	
NORWAY:										
*Communist Party**	X̲				X					
Socialist Left Party									X	
OMAN:										
Popular Front for the Liberation of Oman	X									
PAKISTAN:										
People's Party*(S)										
People's Democratic Party*										
People's Socialist Party*										
PALESTINE:										
Communist Party / People's Party	X	X	X	X	X	X		X̲	X	

COUNTRY Party	90 27th Con	91 Fes	92 Fes	93 Fes	94 28th Con	94 Fes	95 Fes	96 Fes	96 29th Con	97 Fes
Liberation Organization (PLO) / Authority	X		X	X	X	X	(X)	(X)	X	X
PARAGUAY:										
*Communist Party (PCP)**			X	X	X		X	X		
February Revolutionary Party* S										
Free Motherland Movement*										
People's Democratic Party*										
PERU:										
*Communist Party (PCP)**	X		X		X	X	X	X		
Communist Party (Red Motherland)*										
Revolutionary Socialist Party*										
Left Revolutionary Movement* (Castroite)										
Socialist Political Action Party*										
Socialist Party*										
People's Front of Workers, Peasants, and Students (FOCEP) (formerly Maoist / Trotskyist)*										
Front for the National Liberation*										
United Left (*)										
PHILIPPINES:										
Communist Party (not certain if *PKP* or *CPP*, to which National Democratic Front below is connected)	X									

COUNTRY Party	90 27ᵗʰ Con	91 Fes	92 Fes	93 Fes	94 28ᵗʰ Con	94 Fes	95 Fes	96 Fes	96 29ᵗʰ Con	97 Fes
National Democratic Front	X		X							
POLAND:										
Social Democracy of the Republic of Poland (SDRP) (formed Jan 90) S	X									
League of Communists (Proletariat)*										
PORTUGAL:										
Communist Party	X	X	X	X	X	X	X	X	X	X̲
PUERTO RICO:										
Socialist Party*										
REUNION:										
Communist Party					X	X			X	
ROMANIA:										
Socialist Labor Party (PST)					X		X			X
New Socialist Party*										
Party for a New Society (*)										
RUSSIA:[7]										
Agrarian Party					X				X	
Communist Party of the Soviet Union (CPSU) / Communist Party - Russian Federation (formed Feb 93)*	X	X̲	(X)	(X)	X̲	X	X		X	X
Socialist Workers Party*			X	X̲	X̲				X	

---

[7] The formerly Communist Party of the Soviet Union's (CPSU), but now "non-party" (although still communist) *Pravda* has been represented at all the *L'Humanite* Festivals from 1991 through 1997.

Country Party	90 27th Con	91 Fes	92 Fes	93 Fes	94 28th Con	94 Fes	95 Fes	96 Fes	96 29th Con	97 Fes
All-Union Communist Party of Bolsheviks (formed Nov 91)*										
Communist Workers Party (formed Nov 91)*										
Communists League*										
Party of Communists (formed Dec 91)*										
Union of Communist Parties - the Communist Party of the Soviet Union*										
Rwanda:										
Patriotic Front (FPR)	X			X	X	X	X	X	X	
St. Kitts - Nevis:										
Labor Party* (S)										
Saudi Arabia:										
Communist Party	X	X			X					
Senegal:										
Independence and Labor Party (PIT)	X̲	X		X	X	X̲	X	X	X̲	X
Democratic League - Movement for the Party of Labor (LD-MPT)					X	X	X		X	
Socialist Party S					X		X		X	
African Party for Democracy and Socialism									X̲	
African Party of Independence (PAI)*										
Seychelles:										
Progressive Front				X						

COUNTRY Party	90 27th Con	91 Fes	92 Fes	93 Fes	94 28th Con	94 Fes	95 Fes	96 Fes	96 29th Con	97 Fes
SLOVAKIA:										
Party of the Democratic Left (formed Oct 90?) S	X		X							
Communist Party*										
SOMALIA:										
Democratic Front for the Safety of Somalia						X	X	X	X	
SOUTH AFRICA:										
Communist Party*	X		X	X	X	X̲	X		X	
African National Congress (ANC)	X		X	X	X	X	X		X	
SPAIN:										
Communist Party (PCE)	X	X	X	X	X	X	X	X	X̲	X
Communist Party of Catalonia			X	X̲	X		X	X	X̲	X
United Left (IU)					X	X	X	X	X̲	X
Communist Party of the Peoples of Spain (PCPE)		X	X	X	X	X	X	X	X	
African Party for Democracy and Socialism									X̲	
Catalonian Initiative									X	
Workers Communist Party*										
SRI LANKA:										
Communist Party (CPSL)*									X	
SUDAN:										
Communist Party	X	X		X	X	X	X	X	X	X
National Democratic Alliance					X					

COUNTRY Party	90 27th Con	91 Fes	92 Fes	93 Fes	94 28th Con	94 Fes	95 Fes	96 Fes	96 29th Con	97 Fes
SURINAM:										
National Democratic Party*										
SWEDEN:										
Left Party (VP) (formed May 90)	X				X	X			X	
Labor Party - Communists* (believed identical **Workers Party - Communists [APK]**)						X				
Communist Party (SKP)								X		
Communist Party of Marxist-Leninist Revolutionaries (KPML[r])*										
SWITZERLAND:										
Labor Party (PDAS)*	<u>X</u>	X		<u>X</u>	X	X	X	X	<u>X</u>	<u>X</u>
SYRIA:										
Communist Party	<u>X</u>	X	X	X	<u>X</u>		X	X	X	
Arab Socialist Ba'ath Party*										
TANZANIA:										
Revolutionary Party (CCM)	(X)			(X)	(X)					
TOGO:										
Movement for Democracy (MTD)	X		X	X	X			X	X	
CTR (possibly Togolese Resistance Committee)				X						
TRINIDAD AND TOBAGO:										
February 18 Movement*										

COUNTRY Party	90 27th Con	91 Fes	92 Fes	93 Fes	94 28th Con	94 Fes	95 Fes	96 Fes	96 29th Con	97 Fes
TUNISIA:										
Communist Party / *Movement for Renovation (Et-tajdid)* (formed Apr 93)*	X	X	X	X	X	·<u>X</u>	X	X	X	X
Movement for Democratic Socialists									X	
People's Unity Party*										
Unionist Democratic Union*										
Progressive Socialist Party*										
TURKEY:										
United Communist Party (TBKP) / *Socialist Unity Party (SBP or PUST)* (formed 1991)[8]	X	X		X	<u>X</u>	X	X			
Socialist Party of Kurdistan	X			X	X		X	X	X	X
Workers' Party (POT)				X	<u>X</u>		X	X		X
Socialist Party*	X	X								
Kurdish Communist Party*										
Party of Socialist Union of Kurdistan									X	
Party of Liberty and Solidarity								X	X	X
HADEP (Kurdish Parliament in Exile?)								X	X	X

---

[8] The *Political Handbook of the World 1995-1996* lists the TBKP and SBP/PUST as separate parties, but this is believed to be incorrect. TBKP representatives attended only the 1990 meeting; SBP/PUST ones did so from 1991 on.

Country / Party	90 27th Con	91 Fes	92 Fes	93 Fes	94 28th Con	94 Fes	95 Fes	96 Fes	96 29th Con	97 Fes
UKRAINE:										
Socialist Party					X					
*Communist Party**									X	
UNITED STATES:										
American Teachers Federation (progressive tendency)						X				
National Organization of Women				X						
Afro-American Foundation for the Rights of Man				X						
American Caravan of Cuban Solidarity				X						
Committees of Correspondence (CoC) (formed 1991)					X				<u>X</u>	
Communist Party*	X				X					
Social Democratic Party									<u>X</u>	
Socialist Workers Party (formerly Trotskyist)*										
Workers World Party*										
URUGUAY:										
Communist Party (PCU)*	X		X	X	X	X	X			
Oriental Revolutionary Movement*										
Broad Front (FA)*@										
March 26 Movement*										
Revolutionary Party of Workers*										

COUNTRY Party	90 27th Con	91 Fes	92 Fes	93 Fes	94 28th Con	94 Fes	95 Fes	96 Fes	96 29th Con	97 Fes
VENEZUELA:										
Movement Towards Socialism (MAS)			X							
Communist Party									X̲	
Peoples Electoral Movement (MEP)*(S)										
New Alternative*										
VIETNAM:										
Communist Party	X	(X)	X	X	X	X	X	X	X	X
WESTERN SAHARA:										
Popular Front for the Liberation of Saguiel Hamra and Rio de Oro (Frente POLISARIO)	X				X	X	X	X	X	
YEMEN:										
Socialist Party	X			X	X				X	
General People's Congress				X	X					
Arab Socialist Ba'ath Party*										
YUGOSLAVIA:										
Movement for Democratic Liberties					X					
Network of Independent Journalists (AIM)								X		
Social Democratic Party of Montenegro									X	
Social Democratic League of Vojvodine									X	
*League of Communists Movement for Yugoslavia**										
Communist Party*										

COUNTRY Party	90 27th Con	91 Fes	92 Fes	93 Fes	94 28th Con	94 Fes	95 Fes	96 Fes	96 29th Con	97 Fes
New Communist Movement*										
Socialist People's Party*										
Yugoslav League of Workers*										
League of Communists of Yugoslavia*										
ZAIRE:										
Union of Progressive Forces of Congo-Kinshasha (UFPC)	X	X	X		X		X	X̲		
Union for Democracy and Social Progress (UDPS)					X	X	X		X	
Lumumbist Unified Party (PALU)							X		X	
Union of Popular Forces (UCFD)									X	
Lumumba National Movement*										
Lumumba Congolese National Movement - original of Zaire*										
Workers Party*										
Lumumba Democratic Party*										
ZAMBIA:										
United National Independence Party (UNIP)	(X)									
Socialist Party*										

Country / Party	90 27th Con	91 Fes	92 Fes	93 Fes	94 28th Con	94 Fes	95 Fes	96 Fes	96 29th Con	97 Fes
ZIMBABWE:										
African National Union -- Patriotic Front (ZANU-PF)	(X)			(X)	(X)	(X)				
Panafrican Forum	X									
INTERNATIONAL:										
Afro Asian People's Solidarity Organization (AAPSO)									X	
Caribbean Nationalist Movement*										
International Islamic Front Against Zionism*										

Note: The following parties represented at the Refoundation Italian Communist Party (RPCI) Congress of December 1996, just one week prior to the PCF's 29th, were not at the latter: Party of Social Democracy (Cameroon), Forward Revolutionary Force (Columbia), National Revolutionary Union* (Guatemala), National Resistance Council (Iran), Patriotic Union of Kurdistan (Iraq), Communist Party (Kazakhstan), Progressive Socialist Party* (Lebanon), *Congress Party for Madagascar Independence* (Madagascar), National Council of Popular Committees (Martinique), Communist Party (Netherlands) Democratic Liberation Front (Palestine), Socialist Party (Poland), Union of Communist Parties-CPSU* (Russia), Refoundation Communist party (San Marino), Communist Party (Slovakia), Democratic Party of the New Left (Spain), Arab Socialist Ba'ath Party* (Syria), Revolutionary Front for an Independent East Timor-FRETILIN (Indonesia), Kurdish Communist Party* (Turkey), Kurdish National Liberation Front (Turkey), Serbian Socialist Party (Yugoslavia), Yugoslav Left (Yugolavia), and League of Communists* (Yugoslavia).

Appendix III

Final Declaration
of the 4th Sao Paulo Forum

The 4th Sao Paulo Forum held in Havana between July 21 and 24, in the presence of 112 member organizations and 70 observers from the region, was a demonstration of the vitality of nationalist, anti-imperialist, democratic, popular, left-wing and socialist political forces in Latin America and the Caribbean who are committed to profound change in our continent. Likewise, the presence of observers representing 44 institutions and political forces from the United States, Europe, Asia and Africa shows the significance that the Forum has acquired.

The decision during the third meeting, held In Managua, Nicaragua, to make Havana the host of this Forum has become an extremely significant one. It achieved the incorporation of 31 political forces, among them 21 parties and anticolonialist, popular and democratic movements from the Caribbean, which strengthen this united front. Delegates were able to learn about the difficult times Cuba is living through and had the chance to verify the serious effects of the blockade and the systematic policies of aggression that the U.S. persists in applying. Equally, it gave testimony to the steadfastness and will to fight that the Cubans display in their daily struggle to safeguard the Revolution's economic and social gains. When more than 180 million Latin Americans and Caribbeans live in poverty and

88 million endure extreme poverty and destitution, these revolutionary achievements are even more significant.

Because of this the 4th Forum reaffirmed its resolute condemnation of the United States' immoral blockade against Cuba and took on the commitment to step up political action aimed at lifting the blockade and accepting Cuba's full and unconditional integration into the Latin American community, of which it is an indivisible part.

The Sao Paulo Forum has become an unprecedented event. As political forces from the region, representing diverse ideological and political tendencies, we have found ways of moving forward on the difficult but inescapable road to unity in diversity, established In our own historical development consolidated in an ethnically and culturally mestizo continent, the basis of our potential to develop a model, sovereign, integral, just and integrated society.

In the last year, evidently cracks have appeared in the neoliberal project, which until recently had been exerting its influence. The fall from office of the presidents of Brazil, Venezuela and Guatemala demonstrates the strength of social mobilization and a will for change among the people, as much in the field of struggle against corruption as in the rejection of economic policies. Another manifestation of this repudiation was the result of the plebiscite in Uruguay in which 72 percent of the voters showed themselves to be against the privatization of public enterprises imposed by neoliberalism.

The consequences of neoliberal policies are more visible today. We are witnessing the indiscriminate opening of economies; blind confidence in the market, otherwise controlled by oligopolies and transnationals; the organization of the economy in order to guarantee payment of the foreign debt and the subjection to policies defined by the International Monetary Fund and the World Bank. This state of affairs causes the destruction of various branches of industry, especially national industries. It deepens the imbalance between different sectors of the economy, making the balance of trade and balance of payments deficits grow, and, in some cases, dragging economies back to being exporters of primary materials again. In other cases, it leads to neglect of non-export farming while at the same time undermining the possibility of being self-sufficient in food, and above all it increases unemployment and disregards all interest in equality and social justice. In this way, even though there may be growth in some countries, this does not produce an increase in employment, and at the same time it contributes to the growing weakening of nation states, reducing their responsibility for attending to urgent social needs, while national sovereignty is cut back and inequality increases. All of this contributes to the impoverishment of the population.

Poverty is becoming harder to hide all the time. Today, governments and international organizations officially acknowledge this. The 3rd Ibero-American Summit had to add the issue of extreme poverty to its agenda.

The absence economic and social democracy, allied to drug trafficking, corruption, militarism, systems of intelligence and repression on the margins of all democratic control, state terrorism and impunity; are the most serious threats to the building of democratic politics in Latin America.

The Forum emphasized the importance of the struggle for political democracy, understood to be the fruit of the peoples' struggle through the centuries. It confirmed the need to deepen democracy through the combination of representative mechanisms and forms of participatory and direct democracy, integrating institutional struggles with social struggles. Equally, it stressed the need to recognize and incorporate ethnic and cultural plurality and race equality in the exercising of democracy.

The defense and furthering of democratic gains also moves on to the struggle against corruption which has become the everyday practice of Latin American political elites, in their neoliberal and traditional expressions. Corruption is a political and ethical problem which reveals the attempts of the dominant classes to "privatize" the state more and more, subordinating it to the service of their corporate and private interests.

Democracy is incompatible with the continuation of colonialism which subjugates the different peoples of our continent, and with the restrictions to sovereignty and independence that economic domination and foreign policy impose on our countries.

It is obvious that the present state of the economy and politics leads to a constant violation of our nations' human rights, provoking civil outbursts and desperate action, as well as extensive popular mobilization against neoliberalism. Our political forces must contribute to the guidance and organization of social struggles, with an historically significant political outlook.

In order to overcome the challenges set by extreme poverty, the moral crisis, social and political instability and authoritarianism, we must move from condemnation and opposition to proposals and definite alternative action.

Faced with these challenges, and with regard to electoral processes in the rest of 1993 and in 1994, some of the groups taking part in the Forum will run for the presidency or government of their countries in national elections, as for example in Brazil, Chile, Colombia, the Dominican Republic, El Salvador, Mexico, Panama, Uruguay and Venezuela. Clean and democratic elections are requirements that the Forum supports in every case.

For that reason it urges drawing up and implementing development projects which, since they express the interests and organized strength of popular movements, lead on to sustained, independent, environmentally balanced growth with fair distribution of wealth, within the framework of increased democracy at every level.

The crux of this plan is the economic, political and social changes which will allow the bulk of the population to gain access to employment, consumption, property and civil rights. This plan should also avoid the kind of environmental destruction caused by the unbridled lust for money and by extreme poverty.

The formula "grow first, share out later" is unacceptable and a strategy for growth with distribution must be worked out.

The system we envisage implies combining the existence of the market with a state regulatory function--except in the colonies--and the strong encouragement of those structural changes necessary to promote development with democracy and social justice and, especially, to guarantee social programs: education, health, housing, transport, and so on.

We are witnessing increasing globalization of the economy: a development plan cannot ignore this fact. However, in this process the United States is looking to make Latin America and the Caribbean little more than adjuncts to its economy, organized according to the interests of monopoly capital. This once again raises the question of the absolute necessity for continent-wide integration of our peoples and nations.

Integration must happen in the first place within Latin America and the Caribbean as an economic and political process which forms us into a political bloc and increases our strength with a determination to complement and compensate for the differences in our economies. Only a Latin American and Caribbean community of nations, economically and politically integrated, will have the strength to relocate itself independently in a world which is today controlled by large economic blocs and by their policies which are contrary to our countries' interests.

Independence, development, democratization and integration should be neither separate nor consecutive processes but integrated, interactive, simultaneous parts of our economic and political activities.

Integration must include productive activities, political aims and social goals seen from a continental perspective. To accomplish this it is also necessary and viable to promote joint scientific and technical research, sharing human and natural resources and giving access to the advances made by our universities and research centers.

The 4th Forum has noticed that policies of previous administrations continue to hold sway in the hemispheric relations of the current U.S. government. Its military presence in Panama, illegally holding on to the Guantanamo base, maintaining the blockade against Cuba, interventionism, linked or not to the fight against drug trafficking, as well as political and economico-commercial pressures on our countries are among the configurations which must change radically if it is hoped to stabilize an effective new relationship between Latin America and the Caribbean, on the one hand, and the United States on the other. The latter must respect each country's exercising its right to self-determination and, following on from that, the plurality of economico-social systems on our continent.

The Sao Paulo Forum notes that the colonial status of Puerto Rico, French Guiana, Martinique and Guadeloupe and other territories is an unacceptable and continuing reality, and takes as its own the cause of the national independence and self-determination of their peoples as well as recognizing Argentine sovereignty over the Malvinas.

The 4th Forum expresses its support for the efforts the Sandinista National Liberation Front (FSLN), the Farabundo Marti National Liberation Front (FMLN) and the Guatemalan National Revolutionary Unity (URNG) are making in Central America to strengthen the peace processes underway in the area and to implement flexible, consensus policies on behalf of the majority of the population. At the same time it regards the renewal of negotiations in Colombia to reach a political solution to the armed conflict as of the utmost importance and it condemns the institutionalization of an authoritarian and militarized pseudoconstitutional regime in Peru, which in no way helps to solve the serious problems in this sister country.

Furthermore, it supports the struggle of the Haitian people who are on their way to reinstating democracy and constitutionality by reinstalling their legitimate president with no conditions and it warns against using the New York Agreement as a pretext for foreign military intervention in that country.

The Sao Paulo Forum believes it is both valid and necessary to remind delegates that at the very heart of the events prior to the aforementioned conflicts which have held sway with varying intensity in Latin America, are: systematic violation of human rights, dependency, social injustice and atrocities committed by dictatorships, deeds and situations for whose definitive and complete eradication all patriotic, democratic and progressive forces in the Americas must continue to struggle tirelessly.

Finally, on a international note, the Forum declares that we must fight to build a new world order which was described in detail at the 3rd Forum in Managua.

The current international situation among international organizations, which operate according to other world realities, shows itself to be completely unjust and totally lacking in guarantees. The way in which the United Nations and its Security Council are used and the way in which international law is invoked, conditions and erodes the sovereignty and independence of nation states. Under the pretext of seeking legitimate ends the interpretation of principles is twisted, which then operate in the interest of the great powers; at the same time these principles are limited by the military hegemony of the United States. Examples of this are the recent aggression against Iraq, the military occupation of Somalia under a humanitarian guise, the U.S. nuclear threat against Korea and the sanctions against Libya. At the same time the United Nations ignores its own Security Council's resolutions regarding obligations for Israel, at the same time as it becomes an accomplice to the aggressions and the drama which the Palestinian people are subject to in their struggle to establish an independent state.

After the confusions, frustrations and vacuums of the last few years, the 4th Forum took place when popular struggles are on the rise and progress is being made in the search for and renewal of Latin American and Caribbean left-wing thinking.

We are resolved to move forward along new and creative paths of struggle and triumph.

Havana, July 24, 1993.

Appendix IV

Staff of *Links*

[as of July-October 1997, Issue No. 8
(with previous notations)]

Editorial Board	Country	Party (where known)
[Peter Boyle (dropped as managing editor, as of No. 7)	Australia	Democratic Socialist Party]
Dick Nichols (managing editor)	Australia	Democratic Socialist Party
Doug Lorimer (managing editor, from No. 7)	Australia	Democratic Socialist Party
Max Lane (from No. 7)	Australia	Democratic Socialist Party
Reihana Mohideen	Australia	Democratic Socialist Party
John Percy	Australia	Democatic Socialist Party
Andre Brie (from No. 7)	Germany	Party of Democratic Socialism

Lynn Walsh	Great Britain	
Militant LabourMarlin (from No. 7)	Indonesia	People's Democratic Party
Matt McCarten	New Zealand	NZ Allance/ Labour Party
Sonny Melencio	Philippines	MAKABAYAN
Francisco Nemenzo	Philippines	BISIG
Jeremy Cronin	South Africa	South African Communist Party
Langa Zita	South Africa	South African Communist Party
Sunil Ratnapriya	Sri Lanka	Nava Sama Samaja Pakshaya
Carl Bloice	United States	Committees of Correspondence
Peter Camejo	United States	Committees of Correspondence
Malik Miah	United States	Committees of Correspondence
Joanna Misnik	United States	Committees of Correspondence

Contributing Editors

Pat Brewer	Australia	Democratic Socialist Party
[Ernest Mandel, (dec., 1995)	Belgium	Fourth International-United Secretariat]
Francois Vercammen	Belgium	Workers' Revolutionary League
Dulce Maria Pereira		Workers Party
Juan Antonio Blanco	Cuba	Cuban Communist Party?

Jose M. Galego Montana	Cuba	
Cuban Communist Party?Gerson Martinez	El Salvador	Farabundo Marti National Liberation Front
Alain Krivine	France	Revolutionary Communist League
Tamas Krausz	Hungary	Left Alternative
[D.I. Kusuma (through No. 6)	Indonesia	People's Democratic Party?]
Luciana Castellana (through No. 7)	Italy	Refoundation Italian Communist Party
Rina Gaglardi (from No. 8)	Italy	Refoundation Italian Communist Party
Jomo K. Sundaram	Malaysia	
Hector de la Cueva	Mexico	Revolutionary Workers Party
Alejandro Bendana	Nicaragua	Sandinist National Liberation Front
Boris Kagarlitsky	Russia	Russian Party of Labor
Kiva Maidanik	Russia	Russian Party of Labor
Pallo Jordan	South Africa	South African Communist Party
Manning Marable	United States	Committees of Correspondence
James Petras (through No. 8)	United States	Committees of Correspondence

Appendix V

Traditional International Communist Fronts ("Closely Coordinating Nongovernmental Organizations")

Front Name	YBIO* Entry Date	ECOSOC Category[1]	UNESCO Category[2]	Congresses/ Assemblies since 1990		Member- ship (in 000)	Affili- ates	Coun- tries
				Date	Place			
Afro-Asian People's Solidarity Organization (AAPSO)	9/96	II	C	1992 1995	"Lebanon"[3] Hanoi[4]	--	--	76
Asian Buddhist Conference for Peace (ABCP)	1996	roster	C			--	--	17
Berlin Conference of European								

Front Name	YBIO* Entry Date	ECOSOC Category[1]	UNESCO Category[2]	Congresses/ Assemblies since 1990		Member-ship (in 000)	Affili-ates	Coun-tries
				Date	Place			
Catholics (BCEC)	none	--	--	--	--	--	--	--
Christian Peace Conference (CPC)	12/95	II	C	1991	Colakovice	--	--	34
Continental (and Caribbean) Organization of Latin American Students (OCLAE)	10/95	--	--	1995	Santo Domingo	--	25	21
International Association of Democratic Lawyers (IADL)	12/96	II	B	1996	Cape Town	165	--	49
International Federation of Resistance Movements (FIR)	9/96	II	B	1991 1996	Moscow Vienna	Over 5,000	82	29
International Institute for Peace (IIP)	1995	roster	B	--	--	--	--	--
International Organization of Journalists (IOJ)	1995	II	B	1/91 1/95	Harare Amman[5]	--	--	90
International Radio and Television Organization (OIRT)	none	--	--	--	--	--	--	--
International Union of Students	1995	II	B	1/92	Larnaca	--	--	112

Front Name	YBIO* Entry Date	ECOSOC Category[1]	UNESCO Category[2]	Congresses/Assemblies since 1990		Member-ship (in 000)	Affili-ates	Coun-tries
				Date	Place			
(IUS)								
Organization of Solidarity of the Peoples of Africa, Asia and Latin America (OSPAAAL)	2/95	---	---	11/94	Havana[6]	---	---	---
Women's International Democratic Federation (WIDF)	2/95	I	B	3/91 4/94	Sheffield nr. Paris	---	121	97
World Federation of Democratic Youth (WFDY)	1995	I	B	4/91 2/95	Athens nr. Lisbon[7]	---	270	109
World Federation of Scientific Workers (WFSW)	1996	roster	A	11/92	Dakar[8]	500	---	37
World Federation of Teachers' Organizations (FISE)	1995	roster	A	---	---	Over 26,000	152	70
World Federation of Trade Unions (WFTU)	11/96	I	A	11/94	Damascus	135,000[9]	---	127
World Peace Council (WPC)	1995	roster	A	6/93 10/96	Basel[10] Mexico City[11]	---	---	137

144

* Unless otherwise noted, all material here taken from *Yearbook of International Organizations, 1997-1998* (YBIO) (Munich: SAUR, 1997). Organizational listing taken from *Yearbook on International Communist Affairs, 1991* (Stanford: Hoover Institution, 1991), the last of a series. All but the BCEC and OIRT, minor groups in this category anyway, seem to have survived into the 1990s.

Notes:

1. UN Economic and Social Council, *E/1995/INF/5*, September 20, 1995 (for Categories I, II, and roster).

2. UNESCO, *List of International Nongovernmental Organizations*, September 1995, BAX 95/WS.2 (for Categories A, B, and C).

3. *Yearbook of International Organizations, 1994-1995* (Munich: Saur, 1994), Entry #00246. Stated to be a Congress, but the Lebanese city was not given.

4. Ibid., *1997-1998*, Entry #00255. What is reported here is not an Assembly or a Congress, but an Asian Regional Conference. This was the sole event noted in this entry.

5. *Granma* (Havana), February 4, 1995.

6. Neither an Assembly nor a Congres, but an "Encounter of the Right of Peoples to Social Development," presumably the largest meeting sponsored by OSPAAAL in the 1991-1997 period. Ibid., November 19, 1994.

7. *Avante* (Lisbon), February 16, 1995.

8. *Le Soleil* (Dakar), November 11, 1992.

9. *Flashes* (Prague), No. 14/97.

10. *Peace Courier* (Helsinki), No. 6/93.

11. *La Jornada* (Mexico City), October 26, 1996.

Appendix VI

Internationally Active Leftist Labor Unions

The following unions were represented at both the November 1994 Congress of the World Federations of Trade Unions (WFTU) and the January 1996 Congress of the French WFTU affiliate, the General Confederation of Labor (CGT).

Country	National Union	"Repeater" Personnel
Argentina	Congress of Argentine Workers (CTA)	
Belarus	Federation of Belarus Trade Unions	
Brazil	General Workers Central (CGT)	Maria Pimentel (int'l sec)
China	All-China Federation of Trade Unions (ACFTU)	

Country	National Union	"Repeater" Personnel
Columbia	Unitary Central of Workers (COT)	
Cuba	Workers Central of Cuba (CTC)	Pedro Ross Leal (sec gen)
Cyprus	Pancyprian Federation of Labor (PEO)	
Egypt	Egyptian Trade Union Federation	
France	General Confederation of Labor (CGT)	Alphonse Veronese (sec)?
Greece	General Confederation of Labor (GSEE)	George Mavrikos (sec gen)
Guade-loupe	General Confederation of Workers of Guadeloupe	Claude Morvan (sec gen)
India	All-India Trade Union Congress (ATUC) Center of India Trade Unions (CITU) Indian National Trade Union Congress (INTUC)	
Iran	Liaison Committee of Iranian Trade Unions	Hossain Nazari (pres)
Japan	National Confederation of Trade Unions (ZENROREN)	Nobukatsu Owaribe (chief, Int'l Dept)
Kuwait	Kuwait Trade Union Federation	Morshed Faleh al-Wasmi (int'l sec)
Lebanon	National Federation of Workers and Employees Trade Unions (FENASOL) General Confederation of Workers (CGT)	Hassan Hamdan (sec) Elias Abou Rizk (pres)

Country	National Union	"Repeater" Personnel
Madagascar	Madagascan Federation of Workers Unions (FISEMA) Federation of Revolutionary Malagasy Workers Unions (FISMARE)	
Mali	National Union of Malian Workers (UNTM)	
Martinique	Martinique General Confederation of Workers (CGTM)	
Morocco	Democratic Confederation of Workers (CDT)	
North Korea	General Federation of Trade Unions	Li Jin-su (v pres)
Philippines	Kilusang Mayo Uno (KMU)	Crispin Beltran (pres)
Poland	All-Poland Trade Union Alliance (OPZZ)	
Portugal	General Confederation of Portuguese Workers-Intersindical	
Reunion	General Confederation of Workers of Reunion (CGTR)	Georges Marie Lepinay (sec gen)
Russia	Federation of Independent Trade Unions of Russia	
Senegal	National Confederation of Senagalese Workers (CNTS) Union of Senegalese Workers (UTS)	Mabye Moussa (dep sec gen) Djibril Diop (sec gen)
Serbia	Serbian Trade Union Confederation	
South	Congress of South African Trade

Country	National Union	"Repeater" Personnel
Africa	Unions (COSATU)	
Syria	General Federation of Syrian Trade Unions (FGS)	Odeh Kassis (sec gen)
Togo	National Confederation of Togolese Workers (CNTT)	
Uzbeki-stan	Federation of Uzbek Trade Unions	Kudratulla Ravikov (v pres)
Vietnam	Vietnamese General Confederation of Labor	Nguyen Van Tu (pres)
Yugosla-via	Confederation of Autonomous Trade Unions of Yugoslavia	Dragan Radulovic (pres)

International Unions

World Federation of Trade Unions (WFTU)

International Miners and Energy Organization	Alain Simon (sec gen)
Central American Coordinating Committee of Workers (COCENTRA)	Ajax Irias Coello (regional coor-dinator)
General Confederation of Trade Unions in the Commonwealth of Independent States	
International Confederation of Arab Trade Unions (ICATU)	Hassan Djemam (sec gen)
Organization of African Trade Union Unity (OATUU)	Demba Diop (dep sec gen)

Sources:

13th World Trade Union Congress, *Provisional List of Participants* (no further sourcing); "Liste de invites internationaux," *Le Peuple* (Paris), January 4, 1996.

Acronyms

- A -

AAPSO	Afro-Asian Peoples' Solidarity Organization
ABCP	Asian Buddhist Conference for Peace
AKEL	Progressive Party of the Working People (Cyprus)
ANC	African National Congress (South Africa)
APK	Workers' Party-Communists (Sweden)
AUCPB	All-Union Communist Party of Bolsheviks (Russia)

- B -

BCEC	Berlin Conference of European Catholics

- C -

CCM	Revolutionary Party (Movement) of Tanzania
CCP	Chinese Communist Party
CEUL	Confederal European United Left
CILRECO	International Liaison Committee for the Reunification and Peace of Korea
CMEA	Council for Mutual Economic Assistance
CoC	Committees of Correspondence (US)
COMECON	Council for Mutual Economic Assistance
COMINFORM	Communist Information Bureau
COMINTERN	Communist International
CPC	Christian Peace Conference
CPI	Communist Party of India
CPI-M	Communist Party of India-Marxist

CPN	Communist Party of the Netherlands
CPN-UML	Communist Party of Nepal/United Marxist-Leninist
CP-RF	Communist Party-Russian Federation
CPSA	South African Communist Party
CPSU	Communist Party of the Soviet Union

- D -

DKA	Communist Workers' Party (Denmark)
DKP	Communist Party of Denmark
DKP	German Communist Party
PRK	Democratic People's Republic of Korea
DSP	Democratic Socialist Party (Australia)

- E -

EU	European Union
ETUC	European Trade Union Confederation

- F -

FA	Broad Front (Uruguay)
FIR	International Federation of Resistance Movements
FISE	World Federation of Teachers' Unions
FI-US	Fourth International-United Secretariat
FLN	National Liberation Front (Algeria)
FMLN	Farabundo Marti National Liberation Front (El Salvador)
FRELIMO	Mozambique Liberation Front
FSLN	Sandinist National Liberation Front (Nicaragua)

- I -

IADL	International Association of Democratic Lawyers
IICI	International Institute of the Chuche (Juche) Idea
IIP	International Institute of Peace
IOJ	International Organization of Journalists
IU	United Left (Peru)
IU	United Left (Spain)
IUS	International Union of Students

- J -

JCP	Japan Communist Party

- K -

KKE	Communist Party of Greece
KPU	Ukranian Communist Party
KSCM	Communist Party of Bohemia and Moravia
KTP	Communist Workers Party (Finland)

- L -

LCR	Revolutionary Communist Leqgue (France)
LRT	Workers' Revolutionary League (Belgium)

- M -

MPLA-PT	Popular Movement for the Liberation of Angola-Labor Party
MR-88	October 8 Revolutionary Movement (Brazil)
MSP	Hungarian Socialist Party

- N -

NAM	Non-Aligned Movement
NSSP	Nava Sama Samaja Pakshaya (Sri Lanka)

- O -

OAU	Organization of African Unity
OCLEA	Continental Organization of Latin American Students
OIRT	International Radio and Television Organization
OPL	Lavallas Political Organization (Haiti)
OSPAAAL	Organization of Solidarity of the Peoples of Africa, Asia and Latin America

- P -

PAIGC	African Party for the Independence of Guinea and the Cape Verde Islands
PCC	Cuban Communist Party
PCE	Spainish Communist Party
PCF	French Communist Party
PCI	Italian Communist Party
PCPE	Communist Party of the Peoples of Spain
PDS	Democratic Party of the Left (Italy)
PLO	Palestine Liberation Organization
PO	Workers' Party (Ireland)

POLISARIO	Popular Front for the Liberation of Saguiel Hamra and Rio de Oro
PPC	Cambodian People's Party
PPS	Popular Socialist Party (Mexico)
PRD	Revolutionary Democratic Party (Mexico)
PRI	Institutional Revolutionary Party (Mexico)
PSOE	Spanish Socialist Workers' Party
PT	Workers' Party (Brazil)
PTB	Belgian Labor Party
PUCH	Unified (United) Party of Haitian Communists

- R -

ROK	Republic of Korea
RPCI	Refoundation Italian Communist Party

- S -

SACP	South African Communist Party
SED	Socialist Unity Party (East Germany)
SF	Socialist People's Party (Popular Socialist Party) (Denmark)
SKP-Y	Communist Party-Unity (Finland)
SPFWG	Sao Paulo Forum Working Group
SV	Socialist Left Party (Norway)
SWAPO	Southwest Africa People's Organization (Namibia)

- T -

TUI	Trade Union International

- U -

UPRONA	Burundi Paty of National Unity and Progress
URNG	National Revolutionary Unity of Guatemala

- V -

VL	Left Alliance (Finland)
VP	Left Party (Sweden)
VS	Left Socialist Party (Denmark)

- W -

WFDY	World Federation of Democratic Youth
WFSW	World Federation of Scientific Workers

WFTU	World Federation of Trade Unions
WIDF	Women's International Democratic Federation
WPC	World Peace Council

- Z -

ZANU-PF	Zimbabwe African National Union-Patriotic Front

Index

About the Authors and
The Center for Party Development

The Authors

Wallace H. Spaulding, Colonel, USAR (ret.), is a long-time student of international communism. He analyzed international communist affairs for the Central Intelligence Agency for nearly 40 years. His doctorate in international relations is from the University of Pennsylvania. He is also a graduate of the Valley Forge Military Academy and the Army War College and is currently associated with the National Strategy Information Center in Washington, D.C.

Ralph M. Goldman is professor emeritus from San Francisco State University. He is the author of *From Warfare to Party Politics* (1990), has edited *Transnational Parties: Organizing the World's Precincts* (1983), and has written numerous encyclopedia articles on the development of a transnational party system. He currently is president of the Center for Party Development and editor of the newsmagazine *Party Developments*. Dr. Goldman has his doctorate from the University of Chicago.

The Center for Party Development

The Center for Party Development considers party systems essential to democracy and the exercise of popular sovereignty. Through the effective operation of competititve party systems, shared social and political values are reinforced, political conflict is constructively harnessed, and an institutional alternative to warfare is available and supportive of vital features of democracy. Political parties make possible consensual self-governance by human communities.

The Center for Party Development was established in 1992 as a nonprofit corporation. The principal subjects of research, training, and popularization by the Center for Party Development are political party systems in the United States, around the world, and transnationally. The Center conducts research on a project-by-project basis, publishes a unique newsmagazine, *Party Developments*, issues an occasional essay series, *Essays in Party Development*, and sponsors a book series on *Political Party Development* under the imprint of the State University of New York Press.

The Center for Party Development has distinguished boards of directors and advisors. They include:

Directors

Ralph M. Goldman, San Francisco State University, President
John K. White, Catholic University of America, Vice-President
John C. Green, Director, Ray C. Bliss Institute of Applied Politics, University of Akron, Secretary-Treasurer
Charles R. Dechert, Catholic University of America
Jerome M. Mileur, University of Massachusetts
A. James Reichley, The Brookings Institution

Board of Advisors

Rich Bond, Former Chairman, Republican National Committee
E. Mark Braden, Baker & Hostetler, Former Counsel, Republican National Committee
William V. D'Antonio, American Sociological Association
Michael S. Dukakis, Former Governor, Massachusetts
Frank J. Fahrenkopf, Jr., Hogan & Hartson, Former Chairman, Republican National Committe

Donald M. Fraser, Former Member, U.S. House of Representatives and Former Mayor, Minneapolis

Bill Frenzel, Former Member, U.S. House of Representatives

Paul G. Kirk, Jr., Sullivan & Worcester, Former Chairman, Democratic National Committee

L. Sandy Maisel, Colby College

Harold McDougall, Columbus School of Law

William M. Thomas, U.S. House of Representatives, 21st District, California

James A. Thurber, American University

Susan J. Tolchin, George Washington University

(Affiliations for identification only)

Copies of this project report are available from the Center for Party Development, P.O. Box 2656, Kirkland, Washington 98083-2656, USA. Additional information about the Center for Party Development is available on the Internet at http://www.partydevelopment.org.